#1 *NEW YORK TIMES* BESTSELLING AUTHOR

MIKE EVANS

COUNT-

ISRAEL, IRAN, AND ARMAGEDDON

DOWN

TIMEWORTHY
BOOKS

P.O. BOX 30000, PHOENIX, AZ 85046

Countdown
Copyright 2013 by Time Worthy Books
P. O. Box 30000
Phoenix, AZ 85046

Cover Photos: Getty Images

Design: Lookout Design, Inc.

Hardcover   ISBN: 978-0-935199-83-3
       US   ISBN: 978-0-935199-84-0
   Canada   ISBN: 978-0-935199-85-7

Unless otherwise indicated, all scripture quotations are taken from *The New King James Version* of the Bible. Copyright© 1979, 1980, 1982, 1983, 1984 by Thomas Nelson, Inc. Publishers. Used by permission.

Scripture quotations marked NIV are taken from *The Holy Bible: New International Version*® NIV ®. Copyright © 1973, 1978, 1984 by International Bible Society. Used by permission of Zondervan Publishing House. All rights reserved.

Scripture quotations marked NLT are taken from the *New Living Translation*, copyright © 1996, 2004 by Tyndale Charitable Trust. Used by permission of Tyndale House Publishers.

Scripture quotations marked ESV are taken from *The Holy Bible, English Standard Version. Containing the Old and New Testaments.* J. I. Packer, ed. Wheaton, Illinois: Crossway Bibles (a division of Good News Publishers), 2001.

This book is dedicated to my beloved daughter,

Rachel Joy.

FOREWORD 7

1 HOW IRAN LEARNED TO LOVE THE BOMB 13

2 CENTRIFUGE SUBTERFUGE 23

3 CONDEMNATION AND CONSTERNATION 31

4 IAEA: INADEQUATE AND EXASPERATING AGENCY 43

5 EYE OF THE DEVIL 53

6 CONCEALED WEAPONS 69

7 THE CANARY 77

8 ALTERATION OR ALTERCATION? 85

9 CHANGING OR UNCHANGING? 95

10 I SPY! 103

11 A SHAPE IN THE MOONLIGHT 111

12 TWENTY-FIRST CENTURY CYBER WORMS 119

13 LEAVING ON A JET PLANE 125

14 HEL YAM— THE SEA CORPS 131

15 A SEA OF TROUBLES 135

16 COMPARATIVELY SPEAKING 139

17 THE RIAL STOPS HERE 145

18 BLACK GOLD— OILING THE WHEELS OF TERROR 151

19 WAR BY PROXY— FAMILIARITY BREEDS ATTEMPT 157

20 BUT THE PRINCE OF THE KINGDOM OF PERSIA WITHSTOOD ME 165

21 ARMAGEDDON BEGINS 175

AFTERWORD 181

ENDNOTES 184

WHAT IF...?

At 7:31 AM on a Sunday morning in Israel, the prime minister, followed closely by the president of the United States, informed the world that an attack on Iran's nuclear sites had been launched.

The first phase was not with bombers laden with rockets, but with a drone designed to scramble Iran's electrical facilities, Internet, cell phones, television and radio. The disruption to those facilities is being delivered via *Eitan*, an unmanned airliner roughly the size of a jumbo jet with airspeed of approximately 550 miles per hour. Forty-five minutes after its departure, F-15I and F-16I aircraft took off from Ramon Airbase southwest of Beersheba on a secret mission to destroy Iran's nuclear facilities. Twenty-five aircraft have launched at intervals of 10 minutes. With airspeed of about 915 miles per hour, they will reach Iran on the heels of the *Eitan* and in the midst of the electrical disruption.

Israel has jammed radar and communications in Iran with the assistance of U.S. Air Force AWACS and other systems. The president, although not officially informed in order to sustain plausible deniability until the first planes clear Iraqi air space, placed the United States Air Force and Navy on alert several weeks prior. This provided time to stockpile the weapons and aircraft necessary to begin an immediate assault on military targets in Iran.

Upon learning that the mission had been initiated and aware of threatened retaliation by Iran against American bases in Afghanistan, Kuwait, Qatar, Azerbaijan, Oman, and Iraq, and of Iran's declared intention to close the Strait of Hormuz and Persian Gulf, the president placed three Nimitz-class super-carriers on high alert—the USS *Abraham Lincoln*, USS *John Stennis*, and USS *Carl Vinson*.

Armaments on all three carriers include the Mk 57 Mod3 *Sea Sparrow*, the RIM-116 *Rolling Airframe* Missile, and the Phalanx CIWS (close-in weapons system) used to repel anti-ship missiles. The carriers are also home to 90 fixed-wing aircraft and helicopters, including the FA-18 class Hornet which can carry a number of bombs, missiles, and rockets. The combat planes assigned to the three carriers are armed with a variety of weapons effective against military targets including: Bunker buster bombs, *Paveway* laser guided bombs, *Maverick*, *Sidewinder*, and *Arrow* missiles, and the *Mk10 Rockeye II*, a cluster bomb.

In seconds, the status of the three carriers changed dramatically and they are preparing for full-scale war as the president issues instructions that hard targets in Iran are to be attacked. The carriers are joined by the guided-missile submarine USS *Ohio* with a complement of *Tomahawk* missiles and by three Israeli submarines in the Persian Gulf. The 1,100 hard targets, strategic installations that could attack the Strait of Hormuz and/or Persian Gulf allies, including military objectives, mobile missile launchers, missile production facilities, nine active oil refineries, and port facilities at Amirabid, are hit. The strikes against the infrastructure virtually collapse Iran's oil-based economy.

With an arsenal of over 5,000 air-launched weapons Israeli Air Force jets are armed with what is deemed most effective against Iran's nuclear installations—including BLU-109 bunker buster bombs and BLU-113 bunker busters. Israel also deployed the B61-11, the nuclear-armed version of the BLU-113 to destroy the Bushehr and Natanz reactors, as well as target the uranium processing plant at Isfahan, the Russian-built reactor at Bushehr, and the uranium mine at Saghand.

Meanwhile, Israeli Dolphin-class submarines in international waters and outfitted with U.S. Harpoon missiles complete with nuclear warheads fire incessantly at the Iranian reactors. Being readied for service are Israel's *Popeye Turbo* missiles which have been adapted with nuclear warheads. They, too, will be launched from the submarines, if and when needed.

The 16th Special Operations Wing (SOW) stationed at Hulburt Field in Florida has been mobilized and its planes are flying sorties over Iran and the Strait of Hormuz. It is the largest Air Force unit assigned to U.S. Special Operations Command—about seventy aircraft. The 16th SOW is uniquely equipped to undertake missions in Iran and especially its nuclear facilities. Rather than launch a full-scale invasion of Iran, the 16th SOW has hit designated targets.

Fortunately for Israel and the U.S., the strike on Iran's nuclear program has successfully halted the development of a nuclear weapon.

Iran rushed to retaliate with the Shahab-3 weapons still available. Its four anti-ship missile systems acquired from China and fired from its F-4E fighters are also getting a work-out. Its *Sunburn* anti-ship missiles (SS-N-22) from the Ukraine had also been called into play in the Strait of Hormuz. That particular missile has a sophisticated guidance system, but with no nuclear capability, it is limited to a 750-pound conventional warhead. Traveling at Mach 2.2, the missile would completely destroy the slow-moving tankers having no defense against it.

Hezbollah terrorists in Lebanon, Fatah in the Palestine Authority, Hamas and the Islamic Jihad in Gaza have launched some 20,000 retaliatory missile strikes on Israel targeting major cities such as Haifa, Beersheba, Gedera, and the Galilee. Over one-half of the country has virtually been shut down with millions living in bomb shelters. No traffic is flying into or out of Ben Gurion Airport in Tel Aviv; only the military bases are operational. Israel's missile defense systems have been able to counteract the majority of the attacks, but the country sustained direct hits on cities in the north and west. Israeli citizens—over two-thirds of the nation—have taken cover in underground bunkers and bomb shelters as they did during the Gaza War in 2008.

AH-64 Apache and AH-1F Cobra helicopter gunships have been

utilized to target Hamas and Hezbollah facilities using 2000-pound Mark 84 Joint Direct Attack Munitions to destroy headquarter buildings and underground tunnels used to smuggle weapons from one locale to another. Israel Air Force F-15s patrol the skies over Tel Aviv in an attempt to ward off attacks, and U.S.-made *Patriot* missiles, previously employed during the first Gulf War, are being used against incoming rockets. The modified *Patriot* batteries have improved efficiency and allow for the use of the Iron Dome, Magic Wand, and Arrow systems.

Prior to the strike Israel's leaders ordered the combination of all units designated to intercept enemy aircraft or missiles, regardless of range. The multifaceted, operational defense is run by a consolidated administrative center. This also includes early-warning systems and all counter-strike resources. This has helped to protect Israel proper from many of the rockets launched.

Syria, long-divided by civil war, has reunited to retaliate against Israel and troops are amassing on its border. Israeli ground units in the Golan Heights are watching closely for any movement on that front. It is a certainty that as soon as rockets have been moved forward, shelling will begin. Because of the turmoil, oil has jumped to over $200 per barrel as Iran's oil refineries and ports have been completely incapacitated by U.S. missile strikes. Israel and the U.S. are attempting to destroy Iran's ability to fund its terror proxies Hamas, Hezbollah, and the Mahdi army in Iraq.

Seven days after the first strikes occurred against Iran, the world press and various leaders are center stage in an attempt to halt the confrontation. Reports out of Iran signal that its nuclear sites were untouched by the attack, but satellite photos repudiate these claims. Piles of rubble can be seen surrounding the areas where the plants were located.

So, what happens now? The U.S. president has called for a worldwide summit to deal with Israel and has suspended all foreign aid to the Jewish state. The A-Team of fanatical Muslim organizations, Hezbollah terrorists, trained in Iran and embedded in the Mexican drug cartel for years are flooding across the Mexican border near San Diego. They have taken advantage of the tunnel system used to transport drugs to slip into the United States.

These terrorists have been strategically planted by Iran in Jewish population centers. It is thought by the FBI that the operatives will likely begin a systematic assault on Jews in the United States.

COUNTDOWN
10 IRAN

CHAPTER ONE

HOW IRAN LEARNED TO LOVE THE BOMB

There is so much antipathy in the United State regarding Iran's nuclear program, it is difficult to believe the fanatical powers-that-be in what was once ancient Persia received that knowledge through the U.S. "Atoms for Peace" program in the 1950s. Of course, at that time, the Shah of Iran was still in power, and pre-President Jimmy Carter, was still a friend to the United States.

When the Ayatollah Ruhollah Khomeini wrested the Peacock Throne from the Shah in 1979, he disbanded the nuclear program because he felt the weapons research went against Muslim beliefs and legal code.[1] Those restrictions do not seem to bother Iran's Supreme Leader Ayatollah Ali Khamenei. Since Khomeini's death in 1989, and with the ascension of President Mahmoud Ahmadinejad to the world stage, Iran's nuclear program has progressed rapidly. So, how did the world get from "Atoms for Peace" to threatening the destruction of Israel and the United States? How did the U.S. move from "friend" to scion of Satan? The beginning of the end began with Khomeini's rise to prominence.

Who could possibly have foreseen that a grandfather—exiled from Iran to Iraq—would ultimately become the dark, foreboding leader—one who

achieved perhaps the most audacious revolt in history? His rise to prominence and his grasp of power in Iran would deliver one of the most humiliat-
ing blows ever to the United States.

As a child, Khomeini's father was murdered by bandits, leaving him to
the ministrations of his mother and an aunt. Their lives were cut short when
Ruhollah was in his mid-teens. Under the tutelage of his elder brother, he studied the usual madrassa school subjects, eventually becoming a leading expert
in Islamic theological law. It was not until his early sixties that he became active
in politics and began to rally the people against the Shah of Iran.

Khomeini fell in disfavor with the Shah's government in 1963 after delivering a scathing diatribe denouncing the leader's dependence on Western
powers, and particularly the monarch's support of Israel. He was arrested;
freed because of massive demonstrations of support, and finally detained
again in 1964. The cleric was sent first to Turkey and then exiled to Iraq,
where he taught for the following fifteen years.

Eventually, he made his way to France and with the freedoms accorded
by the West he hated, the Ayatollah was able to smuggle tapes of his sermons
to his supporters in Iran. In 1979, Khomeini saw his dream fulfilled—the
overthrow of the Shah—as he descended from an Air France plane onto the
ground in Tehran following the Shah's ignominious departure.

In September of 1979, a group of marauders overran the U.S. embassy
in Tehran and seized fifty-two American hostages. The men and women were
detained for 444 days before being released on President Ronald Reagan's
inauguration day in 1981.

It signaled the end of any and all normal interactions between Iran and
the United States, and was the beginning of the antagonism and hostility that
defines the relationship today. His death opened the door to Iran's renewed
pursuit of nuclear weapons.

When the term "nuclear proliferation" is bandied about in the Middle
East, one name inevitably slips into the conversation: Dr. Abdul Qadeer
(A.Q.) Khan. His name has been closely linked as a leader in the global
propagation of atomic weapons—from North Korea to Iran, and Libya to

Pakistan. Whenever the subject of rogue nations sharing nuclear weapons secrets comes up, the name of A. Q. Khan is not far behind.

Pakistan credits Khan, leader of its nuclear weapons program for twenty-five years, with its forward progress in atomic capability. In 1974, Dr. Khan, an engineer and metallurgist, was invited to become part of the URENCO consortium in the Netherlands that specializes in nuclear research and development.

By 1975, Khan had been invited by the Pakistani government to take control of its uranium enrichment facilities. He made the most of his time in the Netherlands by absconding with blueprints for uranium centrifuges. Once at work in Pakistan, the subversive Dr. Khan began to gather materials and equipment needed to expand the country's nuclear program. He established the Engineering Research Laboratories tasked with the local development of a uranium enrichment facility; he achieved that goal within five years.

By 1983, Dutch investigators would uncover Khan's espionage plot, convict, and sentence him in absentia for the theft of nuclear secrets; the verdict was later overturned on a technicality. By the 1990s, Khan had expanded his clientele to include suspect countries such as North Korea and its rogue leader, President Kim Il-sung. Near the end of the decade, Pakistan officially joined the atomic energy race when its scientists successfully detonated a nuclear device.

It was also in the 1990s that Pakistan's Prime Minister Benazir Bhutto signed a defense pact with North Korea. At that point, it is thought that extremely confidential nuclear expertise was being exported to that country in exchange for the technology needed to build a missile capable of delivering an atomic warhead to a specified target.

Although Iran, not yet a player on the international atomic scene, was interested in securing nuclear information from Pakistan, it was not until 2003 that a secret agreement entered into by Khan in the late 1980s came to light.[2] In that same year, the International Atomic Energy Agency (IAEA) began to press Iran for full disclosure of its nuclear program:

> The IAEA inspection showed that Iran had established
> a large uranium enrichment facility using gas centrifuges

based on the URENCO designs, which had been obtained "from a foreign intermediary in 1989". The intermediary was not named, but many diplomats and analysts pointed to Qadeer Khan. The Iranians turned over the names of their suppliers and the international inspectors quickly identified the Iranian gas centrifuges as *Pak-1*'s, the gas centrifuges invented by Qadeer Khan during the atomic bomb projects.[3]

In March 2001, President Musharraf stripped Khan of his role as director of Pakistan's nuclear laboratory. It was thought that the United States had pressured the government to dismiss Khan because of his ties to nuclear-seeking rogue dictators.

On December 14 of that same year, Iran's second most prominent cleric, Ayatollah Ali Akbar Hashemi-Rafsanjani, spoke at "International Qods (Jerusalem) Day" in Tehran. He issued this warning:

> "If a day comes when the world of Islam is duly equipped with the arms Israel has in possession, the strategy of colonialism would face a stalemate because application of an atomic bomb would not leave anything in Israel but the same thing would just produce damages in the Muslim world."[4]

According to one Iranian newsreader, the call for nuclear arms was one of the strongest by a cleric:

> "It seems that Mr. Hashemi-Rafsanjani is forgetting that due to the present intertwinement of Israel and Palestine, the destruction of the Jewish State would also mean the mass killing of [the] Palestinian population as well.[5]

Perhaps the bloodthirsty ayatollah had forgotten that despite all the efforts of Mr. Khan, Israel had the weapons in her silos of which Iran only dreamed at the moment.

When Libyan strongman Moammar Gadhafi succumbed to international economic sanctions in 2003 and had the country's nuclear program disassembled, investigators discovered that A.Q. Khan also had a finger in Libya's acquisition of nuclear matériel. The U.S. warned of consequences for any further collusion:

> ...after U.S. intelligence officials leaked the news in 2002 that Pakistani enrichment technology was transferred to North Korea, Secretary of State Colin Powell claimed that "President Musharraf gave me his assurance, as he has previously, that Pakistan is not doing anything of that nature.... The past is the past." But Powell put Musharraf on notice: "I have made clear to him that any, any sort of contact between Pakistan and North Korea we believe would be improper, inappropriate, and would have consequences."[6]

In October of that year, Pakistani officials began to genuinely examine Khan's activities. Following quickly on the heels of that investigation, the IAEA issued a warning to Pakistan that possible nuclear leaks had occurred. Research unearthed evidence that several scientists in that program may have sold secrets for personal profit, but President Musharraf strongly denied a government connection. Doubt has surrounded Pakistani protests because of sales brochures produced by Khan at the height of his suspicious activities. One such leaflet touted the sale of centrifuge components to rogue governments.

Perhaps most alarming, some of the documents explained the procedural requirements for reduction of uranium hexafluoride gas to metal, an important step in making a nuclear warhead. The documents included precise technical discussions of how to cast and machine enriched uranium into hemispherical forms needed for warheads. Uranium metal is not useful in civilian nuclear power plants; casting uranium metal into hemispherical forms is a discussion appropriately reserved for the production of nuclear warheads.

There is no lack of nuclear information available to ordinary citizens and terrorist cartels, alike. *The New York Times* printed passages from a sales brochure distributed by Khan Research Laboratories, offering their services on a variety of nuclear issues. The glossy advertising piece bore the "Government of Pakistan" seal, as well as a picture of A.Q. Khan superimposed over a mushroom cloud. The booklet was distributed worldwide.[7]

Khan's terrorists' wish list of products included:

❖ A 'starter kit" for Iraq's uranium enrichment program

❖ P-1 centrifuge blueprints stolen from Urenco (Khan worked there in the '70s)

❖ Advanced P-2 centrifuge designs

❖ Components necessary to build a P-2 centrifuge

❖ P-3 centrifuges

❖ Plans of Chinese-designed nuclear warheads

❖ Almost two tons of uranium hexafluoride (when enriched, the amount is sufficient to produce one nuclear bomb), and information to contact consulting services to advise on assembly and repair

Today, Islamic nations are very close to having their figurative finger poised over the red button. It appears that at least one of these nations may have suitcase nuclear bombs paid for by oil sales to America. In addition to this, the *Washington Post* reported the following on December 21, 2003:

Documents provided by Iran to UN nuclear inspectors since early November have exposed the outlines of a vast, secret procurement network that successfully acquired thousands of sensitive parts and tools from numerous countries over a 17-year period. . . . While American presidents since Ronald Reagan worried that Iran might seek nuclear weapons, US and allied intelligence agencies were unable to halt Iran's most significant nuclear acquisitions, or even to spot a major nuclear facility under construction until it was essentially completed. . . . Iran's pilot facility, which is now functional, and a much larger uranium-enrichment plant under construction next door are designed to produce enough fissile material to make at least two dozen nuclear bombs each year.[8]

When Paul Leventhal, founding president of Nuclear Control Institute testified before the House Committee on International Relations on June 24, 2004, he reported:

> Even if a nuclear-capable Iran was not to provide its terrorist surrogates with nuclear weapons or the materials and know-how needed to build them, a nuclear-capable Iran under its present leadership would be an unparalleled earthquake with shockwaves that could rattle the foundation of U.S. vital interests in the region, at home and around the world.[9]

On February 4, 2004, Khan, the father of Pakistan's nuclear weapons program, appeared on Pakistani television and apologized to the nation for having sold Pakistan's nuclear secrets to other countries. "It pains me to realize that my lifetime achievement could have been placed in jeopardy," he said with an emotion that looked like regret.[10] That same month, Musharraf magnanimously pardoned the scientist who had enjoyed access to Pakistan's most secretive nuclear technology.

This expression of regret was touching; however, the record shows that Khan profited handsomely in his salesmanship. He sold nuclear warhead blueprints and uranium enrichment technology, to the "Axis of Evil" states— Iraq under Saddam Hussein, North Korea, and Iran—as well as to Muammar Qaddafi's Libya.

During the only 2004 Vice-Presidential debate, Dick Cheney uttered these bone-chilling words: "The biggest threat we face today is the possibility of terrorists smuggling a nuclear weapon or a biological agent into one of our own cities and threatening the lives of hundreds of thousands of Americans."[11]

In another development in 2004, American intelligence agencies learned the full details of the coup pulled off by Dr. Khan. In the early 1980's, Khan traveled to Beijing where he obtained the blueprints for a Chinese nuclear weapon compact enough to fit atop a missile. More information about this trip was uncovered that year, following the Libyans' announcement of its nuclear disarmament plans in December 2003.

Also in 2004, the Libyans handed over two large plastic bags of materials that had supposedly come from Khan Laboratories. Drawings inside the plastic bags included plans for a nuclear device that would fit in a sphere about 34 inches in diameter—perfect for rocket transport. Intelligence sources believe that Khan offered his centrifuge technology in exchange for the Chinese bomb design. A missile armed with this small nuclear device would have a devastating effect on any nation in its crosshairs.

Additional documents handed over by Iran relating to the 1987 offer included "detailed drawings of the P-1 centrifuge components and assemblies; technical specifications supporting component manufacture and centrifuge assembly; and technical documents relating to centrifuge operational performance."[12] Furthermore, the documents included schematic drawings showing a centrifuge layout for 6 cascades and a small plant of 2,000 centrifuges arranged in the same hall.

According to an article on "Forum Pakistan":

> Neither Khan nor any of his alleged Pakistani collaborators have yet to face any charges in Pakistan, where he remains an extremely popular figure. Khan is still seen as an outspoken nationalist for his belief that the West is inherently hostile to Islam. In Pakistan's strongly anti-U.S. climate, tough action against him poses political risks for Musharraf, who already faces accusations of being too pro-U.S. from key leaders in Pakistan's Army. An additional complicating factor is that few believe that Khan acted alone and the affair risks gravely damaging the Army, which oversaw and controlled the nuclear weapons development programme and of which Musharraf is still the Commander-in-Chief.

In December 2006, the Swedish Weapons of Mass Destruction Commission (SWMDC) headed by Hans Blix, a former
chief of the International Atomic Energy Agency (IAEA)
and United Nations Monitoring, Verification and Inspection
Commission (UNMOVIC); said in a report that Khan could
not have acted alone "without the awareness of the Pakistani
Government".[13]

Author and former *New York Times* correspondent James Risen wrote of
a clandestine plan by President Bill Clinton's Administration to delay Iran's
nuclear ambitions in what was called "Operation Merlin." He penned:

> ...the CIA chose a defected Russian nuclear scientist to pro-
> vide deliberately flawed nuclear warhead blueprints to Iranian
> officials in February 2000...President Clinton had approved
> the operation and...the Bush administration endorsed the
> plan. Operation Merlin backfired when the nervous Russian
> scientist noticed the flaws and pointed them out to the Irani-
> ans, hoping to enhance his credibility and to protect himself
> against retaliation by the Iranians, while still advancing what
> he thought was the CIA plan to use him as a double agent
> inside Iran. Instead, the book alleges, Operation Merlin may
> have accelerated Iran's nuclear program by providing useful
> information, once the flaws were identified, and the plans
> compared with other sources, such as those presumed to have
> been provided to the Iranians by A. Q. Khan.[14]

CHAPTER TWO

CENTRIFUGE SUBTERFUGE

T he death of the Grand Ayatollah Ruhollah Khomeini fueled the rebirth of Iran's nuclear program. The new leaders moved with all haste and great determination to become a nuclear weapons power. The strategy employed to get to this goal has been both subtle and brilliant.

Iranian physicists decided it was important to study just how Israel was able to launch a military strike against Iraq's nuclear reactor at *Osirak* in June 1981. The Israeli attack was relatively simple because Iraq had only one major nuclear facility. So, Iran's leaders resolved not to make that same mistake. As a defensive move, they decided to decentralize their nuclear facilities. Many sites could be embedded in population centers. Thus, to attack successfully, Israel or the United States would have to launch a multi-pronged strike, more tactically difficult to plan and implement.

Even worse, with nuclear facilities inside Iran's cities, a military strike would cause civilian casualties. Would Israel and America be willing to kill thousands of Iranian civilians to take out Iran's nuclear facilities in a pre-emptive military attack? Clearly, this raised the stakes for Iran's enemies.

Iran's leaders further determined that each separate nuclear installation would be devoted to a single purpose; a piece that could fit into the puzzle. This way, if a particular facility were attacked and destroyed, Iran would lose only the functionality fulfilled at that location. Some operations would be duplicated in other facilities; others might be replaced by out-sourcing to a friendly country, perhaps to Russia, or to Pakistan. No successful attack on any one facility could knock Iran's total nuclear capabilities offline for long.

Since 1988, Iran has opened an estimated 10 different uranium mines. Explorations at these sites throughout the country estimate that the uranium resources of Iran are in the range of 20,000—30,000 tons; more than enough to fuel Iran's civilian nuclear power plants well into the future.[15] In February 2003, Iran announced that a uranium mine was opened at Saghand (Sagend), near the Iranian city of Yazd, in the central Iranian desert of Kavir, some 300 miles south of Tehran.[16]

In September 2004, Iran allowed the international press to tour the uranium mine at Saghand for the first time. Ghasem Soleimani, the British-trained director of mining operations at the Energy Organization of Iran, reported on plans to begin extracting uranium ore from the mine in the first half of 2006. He claimed that "more than 77 percent of the work has been accomplished."[17]

The mine was reported to have a capacity of 132,000 tons of uranium ore per year. The ore is processed into concentrate, commonly called "yellowcake" at a separate Yellowcake Production Plant located at Ardakan, about 60 kilometers distant from Yazd. Iran's uranium processing facility is located at yet another site, Isfahan, a central Iranian city some 250 miles south of Tehran.

The Nuclear Technology and Research Center in Isfahan is said to employ as many as 3,000 scientists, in a facility constructed about 15 kilometers southeast of central Isfahan, at a research complex constructed by the French under a 1975 agreement with Iran.[18] Isfahan also houses one of Iran's major universities with some 1,000 graduate students and approximately 10,000 undergraduates in fields that include science, social science, and humanities.

The Uranium Conversion Facility on the eastern outskirts of Isfahan is a cluster of buildings surrounded by razor wire-topped fencing, and protected by anti-aircraft guns and military patrols.[19] In this facility, yellowcake ore is processed into uranium hexafluoride gas (UF4), the first step required to convert uranium ore to the enriched state needed to run a nuclear power plant or to provide the weapons-grade uranium needed to make an atom bomb.

From Isfahan, the UF4 is transported to yet another facility, this one at Natanz, about 90 miles to the northeast of Isfahan. There the uranium hexafluoride gas is enriched in centrifuges to the higher grade uranium-235. This completes the "full fuel cycle," ending the range of processes needed to get from uranium ore to highly enriched uranium. At lower grades of enrichment, the uranium can be used to fuel peaceful power plants; uranium enriched to uranium-235 can be fashioned into the metallic form needed to serve as the fissile core of an atom bomb.

The Fuel Enrichment Plant at Isfahan is located about 10 miles to the northeast of the town of Natanz, set off from the surrounding desert by a perimeter security fence and military guards. The Natanz Fuel Enrichment Plant houses two large underground halls built 8 meters below ground. The halls are hardened by thick underground concrete reinforced walls built to protect the facility. The construction was designed to house an advanced complex of as many as 50,000 centrifuges.

Experts estimate that the Fuel Enrichment Plant was prepared initially to contain some 5,000 centrifuges, in the initial stage of the project scheduled for completion by the end of 2005 or early in 2006.[20] Operating at full capacity, 50,000 centrifuges would be capable of producing enough weapons-grade uranium to build over 20 weapons per year. When completed, the underground facilities are planned to have no visible above-ground signature, a move designed to complicate precise targeting of any munitions that could be used to attack the facility.

Satellite imagery of the nuclear facilities at both Isfahan and Natanz are available and show the precise location of the operation. The images document various phases of facility construction and concealment, from the time the facilities were first begun, to very recently on a continuously updated basis. Inspection of the satellite images reveals that the complexes are designed to include dormitory/housing facilities for those working at the plant. Also visible are various complexes of administrative and scientific buildings needed to operate the facility.

Even these publicly available satellite images show the military defense and anti-aircraft installations designed to provide security. Inspection of these images makes clear that Isfahan and Natanz are both sophisticated facilities. The Iranians paid careful attention to facility design both for the professional operation of nuclear activity and the military preparedness needed to protect the facilities from attack.

In November 2004, Iranian leaders agreed to stop all processing of uranium at both Isfahan and Natanz. Iran made this decision to comply with a condition set by the EU3 (the European Union countries of France, Germany, and the United Kingdom) for negotiations to begin.

The goal of the EU3 was to settle with Iran the IAEA requirements for facility inspection. The IAEA wanted to determine that Iran was compliant with the provisions of the NPT prohibiting the development of nuclear weapons. The IAEA was obligated to hold Iran to a standard of "transparency," meaning that all Iranian nuclear facilities and operations should be open to IAEA inspection at times and places of the IAEA's choosing.

A "non-transparent" program is one with restrictions on inspections. The argument was that Iran was using those restrictions to conceal nuclear weapons activities. If Iran were allowed to limit inspections to certain times and to certain facilities or particular areas within facilities, the "advanced warning" limitations would give workers the opportunity to "sanitize" operations prior to inspection, i.e., cover up any incriminating evidence.

International skeptics argued that Iran had only agreed to suspend uranium processing because Isfahan and Natanz were not yet complete in November 2004. More time was needed to finish facility construction and resolve technical problems. By agreeing to "stop" operations Iran was truly not ready to begin, its leaders seized the opportunity to appear cooperative. Skeptics argued Iran's primary goal was simply to buy more time.

In September 2004, Iran told the IAEA in a report little noticed at the time that the country planned to process some 40 tons of uranium into uranium hexafluoride gas. This notice tended to be forgotten as soon as Iran announced in November 2004 that uranium processing and enrichment were being voluntarily suspended.

An IAEA report was leaked to the Associated Press in February 2004 suggesting however that Tehran was planning to process 37 tons of yellow-cake uranium oxide into uranium hexafluoride gas, estimated to be enough to make about five small atomic bombs once the UF4 gas was enriched to uranium-235. The report caused a blow-up in the press. Ali Akbar Salehi, a senior advisor to Iran's Foreign Minister Kamal Kharrazi, reacted sharply when questioned about the AP report. "That we want to process 37 metric tons of uranium ore into hexafluoride gas is not a discovery," he told the international press. "The IAEA has been aware of Iran's plan to construct the Uranium Conversion Facility in Isfahan since it was a barren land. We haven't constructed the Isfahan facility to produce biscuits but hexafluoride gas."[21]

This type of forced admission raised concerns in the international community that Iran was deliberately lying about its nuclear intentions. Was Iran going to process uranium or not? The answer to that question was not clear.

Then, in May 2005, international rumors circulated suggesting that Iran had gone ahead with processing the 37 tons of uranium ore, suggesting that work at Isfahan had never been suspended after all. To resolve this conflict, Mohammad Saeedi, the deputy head of the Atomic Energy Organization of Iran (AEOI), came forward. He explained to the international press that 37 tons of uranium ore had been processed, but before formally suspending nuclear processing at Isfahan the previous November. "We converted all the 37 tons of uranium concentrate known as yellowcake into UF4 at the Isfahan Uranium Conversion Facility before we suspended work there," Saeedi told the international press.[22]

In a separate statement, Hasan Rowhani, Iran's top nuclear negotiator admitted that Iran had produced both UF4 and UF6 gas. Rowhani also discussed the suspension of uranium processing in a way that suggested Iran's real intent was work on the Isfahan and Natanz facilities. "It is true that we are currently under suspension," Rowhani commented, "but we conducted a lot of activities in 2004. Today, if we want to start enrichment, we have sufficient centrifuges at least for the early stages, while we didn't have such a capacity 25 months ago."[23]

Rowhani was responding to internal criticism from Iranians who wanted the country to move ahead, hard-liners who had argued that the suspension of uranium processing had harmed Iran's technological advancement. The problem was that Rowhani's statement sounded like Iran was flip-flopping, claiming it had processed uranium before it stopped processing uranium.

Mahmoud Ahmadinejad was elected president on June 25, 2005, and Ayatollah Khamenei, the Supreme (and actual) leader in Iran, had everything needed to take the regime in the ultra-conservative direction he believed would fulfill Ayatollah Khomeini's wishes. Never had the moment been so right for Iran and so wrong for the United States and Israel.

Iran openly resumed processing uranium at Isfahan in August 2005, defiantly breaking the earlier promise to suspend uranium processing while the EU-3 negotiations were proceeding.[24] Iran's leaders were beginning to feel they had the upper hand. Its aggressive defiance was being met by confusion and inaction from the United States and the Europeans.

Officials moved to resume uranium processing at Isfahan, knowing that their unilateral decision would throw a monkey wrench into the U.S. plan to corner them. Yet even here, the Iranians were calculating carefully, taking one step at a time. Re-opening Isfahan meant the Iranians were resuming uranium processing, defined as the refinement of uranium ore into uranium hexafluoride. Though by not opening Natanz, the Iranians technically were not yet engaging in uranium enrichment, defined as the process of converting uranium hexafluoride gas into uranium-235. Carefully, the Iranians were moving their pieces on the chessboard, always with a view to being able soon to declare a surprise "checkmate."

In response, the IAEA fell into a series of crisis meetings. On September 24, 2005, the International Atomic Energy Agency voted at the urging of the United States to hold Iran in non-compliance with the Nuclear Non-Proliferation Strategy. This locked in place a key piece of the U.S. strategy.

When the IAEA vote was taken, Iran was celebrating "Sacred Defense Week," marking the 25th anniversary of the Iran-Iraq war. In Tehran, Foreign Minister Manouchehr Mottaki called the IAEA resolution "political, illegal, and illogical." On state-run television, Mottaki portrayed the

EU-3 as puppets of the United States, claiming that "the three European countries implemented a planned scenario already determined by the United States."[25]

On Wednesday of that same week, John Bolton, the U.S. Ambassador to the UN, told the House International Relations Committee that now Iran had a choice to make. As Bolton explained, "Right now, in the aftermath of the IAEA resolution, it's unmistakably up to Iran to decide whether it's going to continue a policy of pursuing nuclear weapons, or whether it's going to give it up, as did the government of Libya."

Reuters next reported on November 17, 2005, that Iran was preparing to process a new batch of 250 drums of yellowcake uranium at Isfahan.[26] This left no doubt about Iran's intentions. Iran evidently did not want to resume negotiations with the EU-3 if resuming negotiations meant forfeiting the right to process uranium. The Iranian decision was particularly defiant, given that the IAEA was expected to meet on November 24 to vote on the September resolution to take Iran to the Security Council.

Immediately, Russia put a proposal of its own on the table. To break the impasse, the Russians offered to establish a joint venture with Iran to operate a uranium enrichment facility located in Russia.[27] The IAEA postponed a decision to take Iran to the United Nations Security Council for additional sanctions, preferring instead to give the Russians additional time to develop more fully the alternative and to win Iranian acceptance of the idea. Once again, Iran had calculated correctly. By taking the defiant path, Iran had thrown the IAEA and the EU-3 into confusion. Rather than confront Iran, the first impulse of the IAEA and the EU-3 was to retreat, hoping they could still work out a diplomatic solution.

Skillfully, the Iranians had gone from enriching uranium, to not enriching uranium, to maybe enriching uranium, and finally to enriching uranium again, defiantly. They played the same tune over negotiations—first the Iranians refused to negotiate, then they began negotiating, only to defiantly break off negotiations.

Now the Iranians said they would negotiate again, but would not give up the right to enrich uranium in their own country, not even to Russia.

The Iranians would talk, but only as long as the talks were on their terms. With every move, Iran bought more time. With every start and stop, confusion set upon the United States and the Europeans, just as Ayatollah Khomeini had foretold decades earlier.

CHAPTER THREE

CONDEMNATION AND CONSTERNATION

Finally, after more than a quarter century following the 1979 revolution in Iran, Ayatollah Khamenei was gaining confidence that he had mastered the game of international diplomacy. With his team of radical true-believers more firmly in command than ever, Khamenei felt increasingly confident he could get to the end-game and win.

January of 2006 introduced new developments regarding Iran's nuclear pursuits. Israeli defense minister Shaul Mofaz indicated that Israel was preparing for a raid on Iran's nuclear infrastructure. He said Israel could not tolerate an Iran with nuclear weapons, especially given Ahmadinejad's threat to "wipe Israel off the map" during the "World without Zionism" seminar in Tehran.

Condemnation from the West only seemed to strengthen the resolve of Iran's leaders. The world was informed that the Natanz nuclear facility was back online and small-scale uranium—the first step in producing fuel for atomic weapons—enrichment had been added to the mix. In another apparently subtle challenge to the United States, a member of the Iranian parliament suggested to Hugo Chaves, the late Venezuelan dictator, that Iran might assist him in the development of nuclear technology.

The nuclear facility at Natanz was clandestine until the National Council of Resistance for Iran (NCRI), a political resistance group, revealed the site in a press conference held in Washington, D.C. in mid-August 2002. The NCRI press release even disclosed the names of the construction companies that had been hired to start building the Natanz facilities. The press release made public how the Atomic Energy Organization of Iran (AEIO) had set up a front company through which the AEIO intended to pursue the project's needs for facilities and equipment, including such detail as the street address of the fronting company in Tehran.[28] None of this information was known to the UN International Atomic Energy Agency (IAEA) until the NCRI held the Washington press conference. Afterwards, the IAEA investigated and confirmed the accuracy of the NCRI report.

The NCRI on November 14, 2004, issued a press release disclosing a major nuclear site in Tehran that had been kept secret. According to the document, the Iranian Ministry of Defense (MD) had set up "The Modern Defense Readiness and Technology Center" (MDRTC) on a 60 acre site previously occupied by three heavy transport battalions. The NCRI report listed the street addresses of the facility's entrances and described the buildings and installations on the site in detail. The report explained that "activities in nuclear and biological warfare" that had previously been performed elsewhere had been moved to the MDRTC. The press release gave the names of commanders and described how the Iranians had deceived IAEA efforts to investigate.

This was an important report. For the first time, the NCRI gave a full explanation of how the Iranian government had assigned nuclear work to the military, calculating to keep the military operation secret even from Iran's own atomic energy agency:

> The MD and the AEIO are the two bodies that are conducting Iran's nuclear activities in a parallel manner. The AEIO is pursuing the nuclear power stations and the fuel cycle, whereas the MD is seeking to achieve nuclear bomb technology and keeps all its activities secret from the AEIO. For this reason, redoing of works is a major problem in Iran's nuclear

project and many research and preparations are carried out
repeatedly and in a parallel manner with huge expenses.[29]

The NCRI information was obviously obtained from its underground
agents operating in Iran. Much of what was reported had not previously been
known by the IAEA, or by American intelligence units, including the CIA.

Regardless of the State Department designation of the NCRI as a "terrorist organization," what is clear is that the Mujahedeen-e-Khalq or MEK
and NCRI hate the Iranian regime of the mullahs. One of the key weapons
in this unrelenting attack has been information. The NCRI is determined to
expose the lies of the mullahs regarding their nuclear weapons ambitions.
NCRI reports have repeatedly revealed to the world the exact nature of the
clandestine nuclear weapons activities going on in Iran. This does not mean
that all aspects of the NCRI's reports are fully accurate. Still, the vast majority
of what it exposes ends up being subsequently verified by the IAEA or one of
the major intelligence operations run by the United States or other governments around the world. It has provided ammunition for increased calls for
Iran to halt its nuclear program.

On September 2, 2005, the IAEA Board of Governors issued yet
another report concluding that "Iran had failed in a number of instances
over an extended period of time to meet its obligations under its Safeguards
Agreement with respect to the reporting of nuclear material, its processing
and its use, as well as the declaration of facilities where such material had
been processed and stored."[30] The multi-page report listed violations that
went back to 1991, when Iran had failed to disclose the importing of uranium, through more recent violations.

What the diplomatic language took pains to gloss over was the international embarrassment caused to the IAEA every time Iran's deceptions
were revealed by someone else. Third-party disclosures and international
press reports were information leaked from within Iran by internal dissidents. These disclosures forced IAEA inspectors to go back and look for what
they had missed. Finally, the IAEA issued new, corrected reports. The embarrassment to the agency was immediate as the world realized that the Iranians
had fed the IAEA deceptions, half-truths, and outright lies.

Only after the truth was released by opposition groups were Iran's clandestine nuclear activities disclosed publicly. The obvious conclusion was that the IAEA could not be relied upon to do its job.

In a rare move, the U.S. State Department released a set of briefing slides on Iran that were presented to foreign diplomats in Vienna in September 2005.[31]

The whole purpose of the slide presentation was to question whether Iran's pursuit of the nuclear fuel cycle was intended for peaceful uses, as Iran maintained, or for the creation of nuclear weapons, as the State Department contended. The slides were meant to make the argument that the way Iran had constructed its nuclear facilities was more consistent with the way a country would build a weapons program, not a peaceful program intended to generate electricity.

In the slides, the State Department "confirmed a record of hiding sensitive nuclear fuel activities from the IAEA," charging that "Iran's rationale for a 'peaceful' nuclear fuel cycle does not hold up under scrutiny."[32] With Iran sitting on proven oil reserves of 125.8 million barrels, roughly 10 percent of the world's total, plus 940 trillion cubic feet of proven natural gas reserves, 15.5 percent of the world's total and the world's second largest supply in any country, the State Department doubted that Iran needed nuclear power in order to provide civilian electricity.

Even more damning, the State Department argued that instead of spending $6 billion to develop the seven new nuclear reactors Iran proposed to build, it could make the same dollar investments in the country's aging and neglected oil and natural gas infrastructures. This investment would permit Iran to build one or more new refineries, all designed to reduce the country's domestic cost of energy and eliminate the need to import refined gasoline. The State Department slides argued that: "If Iran were to invest $5.6 billion in a high gasoline yield Western-type refinery, it could eliminate its dependence on imported gasoline and increase its annual net oil-related revenue by approximately $982 million."[33]

The State Department slides also showed satellite photographs of Iran's nuclear facilities to diplomats in Vienna. The photos, taken over time, showed how Iran had misrepresented the facilities, and constructed them so as to bury key functions. Some facilities Iran had simply failed to disclose at all. With regard to the gas centrifuge uranium enrichment at Natanz, for instance, the State Department identified the site as "a covert facility in a remote location, which could be used to enrich uranium for weapons."[34] Satellite and ground photographs showed dummy structures designed to prevent detection and identification, as well as facilities that were concealed underground, hardened and well-defended.

Significant progress constructing the Arak heavy water reduction complex was shown for the time period of June 2004 through March 2005. These photos demonstrated that reactor construction was progressing rapidly, despite IAEA Board requests to forgo construction altogether. The State Department dismissed Iran's claim that the Arak reactor was needed for medical and industrial isotopes, a capability that Iran already had inherent in its 10 megawatt Tehran research reactor. The slides also documented development of the uranium mine at Gachin, a uranium mine that was larger and more promising than the uranium mine at Saghand, the only mine Iranian reports had bothered to disclose prior to 2004.

The State Department concluded that Iran's nuclear program is "well-scaled for a nuclear weapons capability," especially when compared to the progress being made in the nuclear weapons facilities of another rogue state, namely North Korea. "When one also considers Iran's concealment and deception activities," a slide argued, "it is difficult to escape the conclusion that Iran is pursuing nuclear weapons."[35]

Finally, so as to leave no doubt, one of the last slides drove home the point: "Iran's past history of concealment and deception and the nuclear fuel cycle infrastructure are most consistent with an intent to acquire nuclear weapons."[36] (The last part of the sentence was underlined for emphasis in the original State Department slide.)

The CIA's "721 Report" released in November 2004 emphasized that Iran's nuclear program "received significant assistance" in the past from "the proliferation network headed by Pakistani scientist A.Q. Khan."[37] This report is named for Section 721 of the 1997 Intelligence Authorization Act which requires unclassified disclosure to Congress regarding the acquisition of nuclear weapons technology by foreign countries during the preceding 6 months.[38]

Suspicion regarding Khan's secret nuclear black market was reinforced on November 18, 2005. On that date, the IAEA released a report disclosing a hand-written one-page document that constituted an offer made by Khan's network to Iran in 1987. The document, which had been voluntarily turned over to the IAEA by Iran, represented an offer to sell Iran nuclear components and equipment. Iran admitted that some components of one or two disassembled centrifuges, as well as supporting drawings and specifications, were delivered by Khan's procurement network, and that other items referred to in the document were obtained from other suppliers.

In July 2005, Iran announced that a solid-fuel engine had been successfully tested for the country's mainstay missile, the *Shahab*-3.[39]

The *Shahab*-3 is a single-stage missile based on the North Korean "Nodong" missile series, with a reliable range of approximately 995 miles (1,600 kilometers), and a maximum range estimated at 1,250 miles, more than enough to hit Tel Aviv in Israel, or U.S. military troops stationed in Iraq. The *Shahab*-3 was first successfully tested by Iran in August and September 2004.

On September 21, 2004, a *Shahab*-3 missile was first paraded in Tehran with banners proclaiming "We will crush America under our feet" and "wipe Israel off the map."[40] The significance of equipping the *Shahab*-3 with a solid-fuel engine is that less time is required to prepare the missile for firing. Anti-missile systems are most effective if they can detect early preparations to fire a missile and if they can hit the missile when it first leaves the launching pad. Missiles in full flight present a more difficult ballistics problem, similar to that of hitting one bullet in flight with another bullet. Also, solid fuel technology generally adds greater reliability and accuracy to the missile's performance. The acquisition of more sophisticated rocket delivery systems makes the situation in Iran even more ominous. Today, Iran's missiles can reach Israel and much of Europe. Within a few years, experts agree Iran's ICBMs will be able to strike anywhere on the globe.

Despite pressure from the EU to adjourn its nuclear pursuits, Iran has continued to defy the worldwide call to halt uranium enrichment. In April 2006, Ali Larijani, secretary of Iran's Supreme National Security Council announced that "if sanctions are imposed on Iran, then we will suspend our relations with the IAEA...If the USA attacks Iran's nuclear facilities, we will stop acting transparently in the nuclear field and continue covert nuclear work at other facilities."[41]

Iran's leaders announced intentions to hasten uranium enrichment by mid-year 2006. A spokesman indicated that it was hoped cascades of some 3000 centrifuges would be established by the end of the year or early 2007. A cascade contains 164 centrifuges linked together. According to the Congressional Research Service, Iran has 18 cascades (2,952 centrifuges) of first generation (IR-1) centrifuges installed in the facility. Iran is feeding uranium hexafluoride into five additional 164-centrifuge cascades and is installing and testing thirteen more.[42]

In typical fashion, Russia reacted to its neighbor's nuclear arms program by rushing to sign an agreement which would provide fuel for a new power plant that opened in 2007. In reaction to Russia's largess, a bill was introduced and approved by the U.S. Congress to sanction any country agreeing to provide supplies or assistance with Iran's quest to purchase "chemical, biological or nuclear weapons."[43]

Iranian President Ahmadinejad traveled to Arak, host city to the Khondab plant, in August 2006 to preside over the opening of a heavy-water plant. The Atomic Energy Organization of Iran (AEOI) oversaw the construction of the heavy water plant at Arak, operated through a fronting company, the Mesbah Energy Company.

The plant was designed to produce plutonium—a major ingredient in the production of nuclear arms. Although Khondab's reactor was set for start-up sometime in 2009, a cloak of invisibility seems to have fallen over the facility since its initial opening. Even though Tehran has indicated that the Khondab reactor is only to be used to produce isotopes for medical use, a major concern centers around the by-product of spent fuel which contains plutonium. It can be used to produce nuclear arms.

The only reason Iran would need a heavy water facility is if the country were planning to build a plutonium bomb. The Russian-built reactor at Bushehr does not use heavy water. Heavy water is required to moderate the nuclear chain reaction needed to produce weapons grade plutonium. Fission bombs requiring plutonium are more sophisticated to design and detonate than bombs using uranium-235. But the explosive magnitude of plutonium bombs is many times greater.

By focusing the discussion on uranium enrichment, the Iranians were telegraphing their decision to build first a simpler, more reliable uranium bomb. Even when the first nuclear bombs were designed by the Manhattan Project in World War II, scientists have known that the mechanics of building a gun-type uranium device were simpler and more reliable. The first atomic bomb ever exploded in combat, the bomb dropped on Hiroshima, was a simple gun-type design uranium-235 atomic bomb. That weapon was considered so reliable that no prototype was ever tested. The *Enola Gay* dropped on Hiroshima a bomb known as "Little Boy." At the time, we did not have a second "Little Boy." Moreover, testing a gun-type nuclear device was considered unnecessary.

Building a heavy water facility at Arak suggested that Iran was on the same path. First, Iranian scientists would build a simple, gun-type design uranium bomb. Later, they evidently planned to be able to build a plutonium device of higher yield and greater destructive power.

In October 2006, Ahmadinejad threw down another gauntlet in his never-ending battle to provoke Israel during the annual Jerusalem Day protest. Not-so-veiled threats erupted as he declared:

"The Zionist regime, thank God, has lost all reason to exist. The efforts to stabilize Israel's fraudulent regime have failed. Believe me; soon this regime will be no longer. The Zionist regime was established in the heart of Islamic territory for one purpose—to pose a threat to the region through constant attacks and killings. This regime has lost its way of existence. Today, there is no reason left for it to remain, and it is about to disappear."[44]

Just days later, Ahmadinejad had another startling announcement for the Western world and for his Arab neighbors:

> "Today the Iranian nation possesses the full nuclear fuel cycle and time is completely running in our favor in terms of diplomacy."[45]

He later told a cadre of Iranian reporters:

> "We will commission 3,000 centrifuges by the year-end. We are determined to master the nuclear fuel cycle and commission some 60,000 centrifuges to meet our demands."[46]

Though handed various sanctions and threats of sanctions, Iran has not waivered from its nuclear arms race. During 2007 Ahmadinejad and the International Atomic Energy Commission danced around each other like fencers exchanging parries and thrusts. The National Intelligence Estimate published in 2007 indicated:

> "We assess with moderate confidence that convincing the Iranian leadership to forgo the eventual development of nuclear weapons will be difficult given the linkage many within the leadership probably see between nuclear weapons development and Iran's key national security and foreign policy objectives, and given Iran's considerable effort from at least the late 1980s to 2003 to develop such weapons. In our judgment, only an Iranian political decision to abandon a nuclear weapons objective would plausibly keep Iran from eventually producing nuclear weapons — and such a decision is inherently reversible.
>
> "We assess with moderate confidence that Iran probably would use covert facilities—rather than its declared nuclear sites—for the production of highly enriched uranium for a weapon. A growing amount of intelligence indicates Iran

was engaged in covert uranium conversion and uranium
enrichment activity, but we judge that these efforts probably were halted in response to the fall 2003 halt, and that
these efforts probably had not been restarted through at least
mid-2007."[47]

The UN Security Council persists in passing resolutions denouncing
Iran's nuclear proliferation; Ahmadinejad and the Ayatollah Khamenei have
continued to thumb their collective noses at its actions. Uranium enrichment
is still a main focus at the Natanz facility. The IAEA indicated in February
2009 that Iran possesses "839 kilograms of low enriched uranium", which
can be further enriched to produce weapons-grade uranium.[48] Estimates
vary on how long it would take Iran to produce a quantity sufficient to make
weapons.

In July 2009, the G8—a group composed of Great Britain, the United
States, Germany, France, Italy, Canada, Japan and Russia—met in L'Aquila,
Italy. One of the topics discussed was Iran's nuclear program. A communiqué
issued by the leaders defined their concerns regarding the rogue country, but
stopped short of taking a definitive stand:

> "We remain deeply concerned over proliferation risks
> posed by Iran's nuclear programme. We strongly urge Iran
> to co-operate fully with the International Atomic Energy
> Agency and to comply with the relevant UN Security Coun-
> cil resolutions without further delay."

The IAEA points out that questions regarding Iran's military utilization
of its program have gone unanswered, and Iran continues to defy global
demands to halt its quest for nuclear capabilities. Could there have been
something behind Ahmadinejad's rabid defiance other than his megaloma-
niacal tendencies? It is no mystery that Iran's former president is a fanatical
Shia *Twelver.* He is a follower of the twelfth Imam otherwise known as the
Mahdi. At the age of five, this last descendant of Muhammad was supposedly
hidden away in a state often called "occultation." His followers believe that

through some apocalyptic event—in the midst of turmoil and warfare—the Mahdi will be revealed and will establish a worldwide caliphate with Shia Islam at its center.

Ahmadinejad is such a rabid follower he has claimed to have been contacted by the Mahdi—much to the chagrin of some of the clerics in Iran. Why does belief in the Mahdi make any Iranian leader so dangerous? According to Shia theology, only Allah has the knowledge of when the Mahdi will return to Qom, a city southwest of Tehran. That in the company of Jesus, the Mahdi will travel along the new roads constructed under Ahmadinejad's auspices to the capital, Tehran, where he will assume his rightful role as worldwide caliph.

Iran's Supreme Leader Ali Khamenei is not a follower of the *Twelver* sect, but has chosen to elevate a man, not once but twice, who is militant in his faith. Iran's former president believed he could create the catastrophic circumstances which would bring the Mahdi forth. His conviction was made even more menacing with each new revelation regarding nuclear advancements. An assault on either Israel or the United States would launch retaliatory measures which would have, in Ahmadinejad's book, brought about the chaos necessary to unleash the Mahdi on the world.

America's forty-fourth president has all but acquiesced to Iran's nuclear course. Even during the election process, Mr. Obama signified that he was agreeable to a meeting with the regime without preconditions, a move taken to be weakness on the part of the American president. Before he left office, Ahmadinejad declared the issue closed, not worthy of talks with the leader of "The Great Satan." He has rebuffed the advances of a man who apparently wants to dance with Iran.

Ahmadinejad felt he was in the driver's seat and that unless a backbone transplant was in the offing, Mr. Obama would find it difficult, if not impossible, to engage the leaders in Iran from a position of weakness.

If, or more accurately, when Iran acquires a nuclear device, it could well be the impetus for other Arab countries in the Middle East to follow suit. Even now, the race is on to build reactors in Jordan, the UAE, and Abu Dhabi for the production of nuclear power stations. Egypt, like Jordan, has a treaty in place with Israel to build a reactor. Britain has inked an agreement with Jordan; the U.S. with the UAE (a country with strong ties to Iran), and France has signed a multi-billion dollar agreement with Abu Dhabi which will, in the words of David Miliband, British Foreign Secretary, "move the world to a low-carbon economy." He added that nuclear power needs to be a strong part of the mix.[49] Russia, not wanting to be left out, is courting Egypt with its nuclear stores.

Currently, Israel is the only country in the Middle East with nuclear capabilities. The world is waiting to see if the Israelis will halt the nuclear arms race by attacking Iran's nuclear reactors. If not, the balance of power may shift to its Arab neighbors who fear Iran's global intentions.

CHAPTER FOUR

IAEA: INADEQUATE AND EXASPERATING AGENCY

irector General Mohamed El Baradei, head of the IAEA reported in September 2009 that Iran was guilty of not revealing the uranium enrichment site at Qom. Despite that accusation, the agency also reported that there was insufficient evidence to aver unequivocally that Iran had a viable nuclear program.[50]

Qom is a particularly relevant site to many *Twelvers* in Iran; it is near there that the Jamkaran Mosque is located. In my interview with Israeli Lt. General Moshe Ya'alon, he indicated another reason for Iran's hostile determination to produce nuclear weapons:

"Shiite Muslims believe that the Twelfth Imam, or Mahdi, the last in a line of saints descended from Ali, the founder of their sect, vanished down a well (near Jamkaran, Iran) in 941 A.D. According to their beliefs, the Mahdi went into a state of 'occultation,' like the sun being hidden behind the clouds. After a stormy period of apocalyptic wars, the clouds will part, and the sun (the Mahdi) will be revealed. They believe that when he is released from his imprisonment, the entire world will submit to Islam."[51] These words would not have been so startling—except they fell from General Ya'alon's lips.

Each Tuesday evening in Qom, crowds of Shi'a pilgrims and clerics

gather at the well at Jamkaran down which it is thought the Mahdi disap-
peared. There they pray and write notes to the Imam asking for help; the
notes are dropped into the well. Having become hypersensitive to its image
in foreign countries, the administrators at Jamkaran have restricted foreign
access to both the mosque and the well.

When Mahmoud Ahmadinejad ran for president of Iran in 2005, his
chief spiritual advisor, Ayatollah Mohammad Taqi Mesbah Yazdi told believers that Ahmadinejad was the "chosen" of the Mahdi. Because Ahmadinejad
is the person designated to prepare the way for the Twelfth Imam's second
coming, Yazdi told followers they had a duty to vote for him.[52] Not surpris-
ingly, when Ahmadinejad became president, he reportedly allocated $17 mil-
lion to the Jamkaran Mosque for renovations.

With renewed focus on the enrichment site at Qom, in November 2009,
the IAEA's board of governors was petitioned by the United States, China,
Russia, and three other nations to demand that Iran stop work on the facility and halt enrichment. Iran defied the order under IAEA threats of further
sanctions. [53]

While feigning indignation, the UN agency gave Iran a lax tap on the
wrist for "failing to explain purchases of classified technology and clandestine
trials of 'high-precision detonators and modified designs of missile cones'"[54]
to hold larger loads. True to an avowal to continue its nuclear low-enrich-
ment program, Iran had produced more than 2.5 metric tons of uranium,
enough to produce two weapons. All the time, the leaders of the country
declined to respond to questions regarding its activities. By July 2010, IAEA
inspectors had been barred from Iran. One month later, a second cascade
of centrifuges were put online at a site in Natanz. A 20 percent increase in
production was noted.

By November 2011, an IAEA report uncovered sound indications that
some progress had been made in designing a viable nuclear bomb. Agency
Director Yukiya Amano stated that information gathered by the agency indicated "that Iran has carried out activities relevant to the development of a
nuclear explosive device."[55] Iran, of course, charged the United States with
coercion in order to bring to bear an unjustified political impact.[56] It was also

during that same month that news of Parchin—an Iranian military base—
and the possibility of a "large explosive containment vessel"[57] reached IAEA
inspectors' ears. The inspectors were cleared to travel to Iran before the end
of 2012 to inspect the Parchin test facility. Their aim was to confirm whether
Iran has expanded its research specifically on the acquisition of a nuclear
bomb for military use. Enough time has elapsed since the request was first
made to Iranian leaders that images from space satellites indicate all traces of
nuclear activity have been cleansed from the site. Buildings have been razed
and soil has been carted away in an obvious attempt to deceive the inspectors. Access to the site was denied on the basis that it had "no connection
with Iran's nuclear activities."[58]

Even though Iran has boasted of raising the number of cascades—a
large number of connected centrifuges for the enrichment of uranium—the
design of those employed in that country's nuclear program at Natanz and
Fordow are thought to be both outdated and erratic in operation. Nuclear
expert Mark Fitzpatrick pointed out that Iran had been working on "second-
generation models for over ten years now and still can't put them into large-
scale operation".[59]

In a report released by the IAEA in May 2012, concerns were raised that
Iran had reached the point of having enriched enough uranium to produce a
nuclear weapon and especially at the Fordow facility where levels had been
tested at 27 percent. Previously the highest level was determined to be 20
percent.

By August of that year a report indicated that Iran had twice the number
of centrifuges online deep underground at Fordow. Associated Press articles
indicated that Iran had performed work with enhanced computer models of
a viable nuclear warhead. This stage of nuclear development often goes hand-
in-hand with actual trials of the equipment in question—nuclear components.
Once again the IAEA responded forcefully! It passed yet another useless resolution calling for inspections of Iran's various nuclear facilities. The only good
news at that point was that the declaration was supported by China, France,
Germany, Russia, the United States, and the United Kingdom.[60]

By the end of 2012, there had been no moves to allow the UN inspection agency access to any sites inside Iran's borders. Added to that denial was a report that the reactor at Arak was due online in early 2014.

While the world waits, the IAEA continues to prove that it is but a toothless tiger on the world stage. Repeated efforts to gain access to Iran's nuclear facilities in an attempt to enforce nuclear compliance have failed. As late as December 2012, Yukiya Amano, the organizations' head reported:

> "We have intensified our dialogue with Iran this year, but no concrete results have been made yet. What we are asking in the negotiations is to have access to sites, information and people."[61]

As the clock ticked down to January 1, 2013, Iran's uranium enrichment potential did not improve: An additional 2,255 centrifuges were online at Natanz. Fordow, near Qom, boasted 2,710 centrifuges capable of producing 19.75 percent enriched uranium. Iranian officials continue to deny the IAEA access to Parchin.

In the spring of 2013, President Barack Obama made his first official visit to Israel. During a joint press conference with Prime Minister Benjamin Netanyahu, the question of Iran's nuclear pursuits was introduced. Netanyahu reminded the president:

> "Notwithstanding our joint efforts and your great success in mobilizing the international community, diplomacy and sanctions still have not stopped Iran's nuclear program." He added that the diplomatic approach must be "augmented by clear and credible threat of military action...I know that you appreciate that Israel can never cede the right to defend ourselves to others, even to the greatest of our friends.""[62]

Moshe Ya'alon, Israel's Deputy Prime Minister, who also holds the portfolio of Strategic Affairs Minister, has long averred that Israel must develop a "credible military option" in order to confront Iran's nuclear program. Ya'alon believes that Israel must have a genuine, practicable, and efficient option. He has indicated that Iran needs to fear the reality and usefulness of Israel's military options.

Recent revelations indicate that Iran is no longer fearful of retaliation from any source—U.S. or Israeli. Iranian leaders continue to threaten world peace without fear of retribution. Certainly there has been no indication that President Obama and his administration are willing to do anything proactive to halt Iran's march toward securing nuclear weapons. Once that has been accomplished, no part of our planet could avoid Iran's murderous crosshairs.

Perhaps the most frightening aspect of the situation in the Middle East is the threat of nuclear war. Arab nations have a simple philosophy of nuclear warfare: The Muslim world, with its six million square miles of land and millions of soldiers, can absorb a massive nuclear attack and still survive; Israel cannot.

In the spring of 2013, another specter arose—another option for Iran to fulfill its nuclear vision: The purchase of a completed bomb from North Korea. The rogue state on the Korean Peninsula has completed three successful nuclear tests. The success of those operations would give the mullahs of Tehran atomic weapons not in months or years, but in hours! Most of Iran's missile technology is based on work done by China and North Korea. With an escalating crisis in Korea, a few analysts are studying the possibility of Iran buying already completed nuclear weapons from North Korea that would fit on Iran's existing missiles and be ready for use immediately.

A report from the Institute for Science and International Security provided information regarding North Korea's nuclear track:

> Little is known about North Korea's ability to make a deliverable nuclear weapon, although it is likely able to build a warhead, perhaps one of mixed reliability, which can fit atop a Nodong missile with a range of less than 800 miles. Its declaration of two kilograms in its 2006 test would imply that it knows far more about making nuclear weapons than commonly believed, assuming that the statement is not a bluff. Moreover, North Korea has worked on nuclear weaponization for over 20 years, supporting assessments that it can build a warhead for a Nodong missile.

Accepting North Korea's statements about the size of its stock of separated plutonium, or currently 34-36 kilograms, it is possible to estimate the number of nuclear weapons it could build. Assuming that each weapon contains about 2-5 kilograms of plutonium, North Korea could build anywhere from 6 to 18 nuclear weapons. This broad range reflects uncertainties in the amount of plutonium North Korea needs in each weapon. The midpoint is 12 nuclear weapons, where the warheads contain on average about three kilograms of plutonium.[63]

It is impossible to overstate how serious a threat an alliance between the two "Evil Empires" would quickly become. When North Korea successfully conducted its third nuclear test, top Iranian nuclear scientists were present as observers. Iran has billions in oil wealth, and North Korea desperately needs the money to feed its starving people and build up its military forces. The warheads could be placed on a cargo plane and flown to Iran in a matter of hours. Once there, they could quickly be assembled and Iran would have ready-to-use nuclear weapons. This is a match made in hell—and it poses a danger to Israel that seems completely overlooked by most of the world.

It has become more and more apparent that Israel cannot necessarily rely on the United States to come to her aid in the face of a credible nuclear threat. Given the United States' less than stellar role in Iraq and Afghanistan and the uptick in North Korea's saber rattling, Iran could be the least of worries—unless the baby-faced Korean dictator, Kim Jong Un, and the Supreme Leader of Tehran should elect to join forces. In reality, at any given moment a flashpoint could occur that would send the world into an unthinkable and yet terrible inevitability.

Neither Iran nor North Korea is constrained by what, during the Cold War of the twentieth century, was called MAD, "mutual assured destruction." The theory behind this policy is that each superpower engaged in the Cold War, i.e., Russia and the US, was sufficiently armed to destroy the other in the event of an attack. The outcome of such an event would bring about the near total destruction of both countries.

This theory was directly responsible for the nuclear arms race that was unleashed during the late '40s, and lasted through the mid-1980s. Both nations had sufficient incentive not to engage in a direct nuclear conflict, and both were content to employ proxy wars around the world. Could it have been this "proxy war" concept that gave Iran the idea of stationing groups such as Hezbollah and Hamas in Lebanon and Gaza, and to send proxies into Iraq to foment upheaval in that country? Iran's leaders have not been shy about taking credit for the influx of missiles into Gaza:

> At a November 2012 Basij conference in Mashhad, Majlis member Javad Karimi, a former IRGC official, said: "We sent the besieged Gaza 50,000 missiles and thousands of anti-tank rockets, because if we do not defend [Gaza], we will suffer casualties in the streets of Mashhad." He added: "Launching Fajr-5 missiles at the center of Tel Aviv attests to a major victory in the conflict over Palestine in favor of the Iranian nation, and allowed Iran to once again prove its strength to the world. These 50,000 Fajr missiles show the crucial role Iran played in Gaza's victory."[64]

And in another admission:

> Ali Akbar Velayati, advisor to Supreme Leader Ali Khamenei for international affairs, said: "[Palestinian Islamic Jihad leader] Ramadan 'Abdallah [Shalah] said to me: 'We want to strike Tel Aviv with Fajr-5 missiles,' [but] one of the revolutionaries in North Africa said: 'You can strike any place you want but not Tel Aviv.' But we did it, and three million Zionists ran to bomb shelters in fear."[65]

Perhaps the most pressing question after all is not when will Iran have the bomb, but rather will its mad leaders be deterred by "mutual assured destruction?" Or do they, like Khomeini, believe "let Iran go up in smoke, provided Islam emerges triumphant in the rest of the world"?[66]

General Yossi Peled, commander of Israel's northern divisions in the recent fighting between Israel and Hezbollah said this about Iran having nuclear weapons:

> If this moment comes that Iran has nuclear ability, let's say they decide to make a move in the Middle East to free it from the bad influence of the West. They would take Egypt, Israel, Lebanon, it's against the interests of the Western world, and against the U.S. Don't you think it will limit the reaction of the U.S.? Everything will change. I wish to be wrong, but I don't feel so. The second point is that they think in a different way than you and me and most of the Western world. Maybe they will be ready to sacrifice half of the Islamic world to destroy half of the Western world. It's possible because they think a different way, a different religion; a different mentality. And already, they are strong enough to convince their people it is okay to sacrifice a million to achieve control.

Professor Raymond Tanter, a National Security advisor under Reagan/ Bush and one of the founders of the Iran Policy Committee, saw that the Islamofascist extremism and nuclear weapons is a mix the west truly can't sit by and allow to happen:

> What difference does it make if an Islamofascist regime gets nuclear weapons? It would be a huge boost to the government of Iran in terms of its coercive diplomatic ability to coerce the neighbors; it would accelerate the arms race in the Middle East where Saudi Arabia, Egypt, and Israel will either acquire or make explicit their nuclear weapons. The threat from Iran is a huge destabilizing factor in U.S.-European relations.
>
> So what then is the nation prepared to do? I say go ahead and try diplomacy but realize that when you are dealing with an Islamofascist regime, diplomacy is unlikely to work.

Why not? Because the Islamofascist regime is not a normal regime where you make cost benefit calculations, where you make proposals and counter-proposals, you make compromises. This regime doesn't negotiate in the same manner that a western government would negotiate. Hence you should try diplomacy, but be prepared for diplomatic failure and have options other than military options. That's what I call regime change; by empowering the Iranian people through their opposition groups.[67]

Khomeini's radical Islamic belief system brainwashed into the mind of every Islamic fanatic is never more apparent than in various attacks around the world that killed U.S. Marines, sailors, and troops in Iraq, but has also took the lives of innocent bystanders, frequently Muslims. The Iranian-backed death squads in Iraq have no compunction about blowing themselves up in crowded marketplaces, outside schools, in busy city centers, all the while shouting, "*Allah akbar!*"

According to former Palestinian terrorist Walid Shoebat:

He would sacrifice his whole country. When somebody reaches to the tyranny of Islamic Fundamentalist like Ahmadinejad, his people don't matter, just like Hitler. The people do not matter. They're just elements to establish a goal. With Islamic Fundamentalism and Nazism, two things are very similar. The end justifies the means, and there is no respect for borders.[68]

Apparently in the fanatical Islamic mindset, it is okay to kill Muslim brothers for they will attain heaven; the hated infidel will, however, go to their reward in hell. For the radical *Jihadists*, the end justifies the murders of innocent Muslim passersby because, after all, they will attain their reward that much sooner. Sadly, young Iranian students are literally brainwashed by textbooks found in their schools. The youngsters are taught that to sacrifice themselves as martyrs for the "cause" is the ultimate goal, and they must be ready at all times to attain that goal.

John R. Bolton, then-Under Secretary for Arms Control and International Security, said in August 2004:

> What we ask for is not much—only what is necessary to protect our security and to prevent Iran from developing nuclear weapons and other WMD. All that Iran must do is to abide by the treaties it has signed banning weapons of mass destruction and stop its program to develop ballistic missiles. We cannot let Iran, a leading sponsor of international terrorism, acquire nuclear weapons and the means to deliver them to Europe, most of central Asia and the Middle East, or beyond.[69]

Without serious, concerted, immediate intervention by the international community, Iran may well be too far along the road to achieving its stated purpose.

CHAPTER FIVE

EYE OF THE DEVIL

The world is over a decade into the twenty-first century. At the end of the twentieth century Americans could look back on the halting of the Cold War, the collapse of the Berlin Wall, the end of the first Persian Gulf War, and a time of prosperity. As the clock struck midnight on New Year's Eve, December 31, 1999, we discovered that a catastrophe had been averted. The world had not come to a standstill either technologically or mechanically. Folks did not need to hole up in their homes with shelves of canned goods and bottled water, and with weapons in hand to protect their property from the midnight marauders of a new millennium. It was, surprising to many, business as usual.

However, the eyes of our enemies never strayed from their focus upon us; they simply waited to determine our next move. Despite the tragic warning of 9/11 and the certainty that there are those out there who only want to see us dead, we have too quickly and easily returned to the monotony of everyday life and the belief that we are somehow immune to another devastating terrorist attack.

When I see such apathy, I am reminded of an encounter I had with Isser Harel, the head of Mossad (Israeli Intelligence—from 1947-1963) at a dinner in his home a few months before the September 23, 1980 presidential election. That night I asked Harel, "Who do you think will be America's next president?"

Harel responded, "The word on the streets is that terrorists might have a say about that. They are going to attempt to influence your elections by offering to release the hostages precisely when Reagan is sworn into office."

Completely stunned, I responded, "What? Why?"

Harel said, "They want Carter out because of his challenges to Islam." The former intelligence officer was referring to the Camp David accords, and to Carter's insistence that Sadat give a speech in Egypt stating that religion and politics must be separate. This speech was heard by a blind cleric named al-Rahman who issued the *Fatwa* to assassinate Sadat; the same cleric later indicted for his part in the first bombing of the World Trade Center in 1993.

We talked about America's foreign policy and tensions in the Middle East, Saddam Hussein's power-play in Iraq, and how Carter manipulated the overthrow of the Shah of Iran through the American embassy in Tehran — contrary to the advice of Israeli intelligence. Mossad asserted that instead of improving the country it would give impetus to Islamic fundamentalists and provoke the Soviets to invade Afghanistan.

"They want to kill Sadat," Harel said. "And now, they want to kill Carter's chances of reelection. They feel that if the hostages are released early, it would put Carter back in office."

Later on that same evening, I asked Harel another question: "Will terrorism ever come to America?"

"Will terrorism come to America?" He repeated my question back to me. "America is developing a tolerance for terrorism. America has the power to fight terrorism but not the will; the terrorists have the will, but not the power. But all of that could change in time. Oil buys more than tents. You in the West kill a fly and rejoice. In the Middle East, we kill one, and one hundred flies come to the funeral.

"Yes, I fear America will experience terrorism in time."

"Where will it come?" I asked him.

He thought for a moment. "New York is the symbol of your freedom and capitalism. It's likely they will strike there first. At your tallest building [at that time the Empire State Building], which is a symbol of your power."

Little did I know that both of Harel's predictions—the release of the hostages at the exact hour of President Reagan's inauguration and the terrorist strikes against the tallest building in New York—would come to pass within a dozen years. And less than a decade after that the United States would plunge headfirst into an apocalyptic tornado on September 11, 2001.

There are many who think the West cannot survive the onslaught of fanatical Islam of which Iran is only one, but the primary, example. In spite of the tremendous upheaval we are witnessing with the rise of terrorism worldwide, we fail to recognize the danger. Surrounded by those who wish to see both America and Israel wiped off the map, one must ask: How can the West be saved?

Just as the world in Hitler's day did not recognize the process by which that cruel dictator began to dehumanize the Jews in Europe, so it does not recognize that Iran has, for decades, been using those same guidelines to question the legality of the State of Israel, and the proprietary claim of the Jewish people to that small spot in the Middle East. The Supreme Leader, Ayatollah Ali Khamenei has questioned:

> Who are the Israelis? They are responsible for usurping houses, territory, farmlands and businesses. They are combatants at the disposal of Zionist operatives. A Muslim nation cannot remain indifferent vis-à-vis such people who are stooges at the service of the arch-foes of the Muslim world."[70]

Khamenei's intent toward Israel cannot be more obvious than in his following statement printed in London's *Daily Telegraph*:

> There is only one solution to the Middle East problem, namely the annihilation and destruction of the Jewish state.[71]

One of the most powerful things that can save the West is a policy of zero-tolerance to terrorism. After Harel's warning, it became clear to me that America did, indeed, have a tolerance for terror. Today, it is still operating under that policy. Iran was responsible for more deaths through IEDs and the injuring of more American soldiers than anyone else in Iraq. Through its proxies, Hezbollah and Hamas, it is responsible for killing more Jews in the State of Israel than any other supporter of organized terror, and still U.S. presidents have sidestepped that issue when trying to coerce Israel to the bargaining table.

Syria, too, is in the business of terror. It allows Iran to fly its planes into Syrian air space in order to arm Hezbollah and Hamas. The U.S. must immediately establish a policy by which it will not, under any circumstances, negotiate with any regime that supports, aids or funds terror. That includes the PLO, Syria, Iran, and virtually any nation aligned with radical Islam. A zero-tolerance policy will shut down the engine of terror. All diplomatic relations with terror-supporting states need to cease. The diplomatic missions for those countries in the U.S. need to be closed, and the harshest penalties imposed for sustaining terrorist factions. They should be isolated from the world.

In addition, the U.S. government must stop the hypocrisy of Jew-baiting. It's appalling for the U.S. to continually promise Muslim, Jew-hating bigots an Islamic state with its capital in Jerusalem. An ironclad bond needs to be established between Israel and the U.S., with Jerusalem recognized as Israel's undivided capital, and Judea and Samaria acknowledged as Israel's land.

A secure and strong Israel is in America's self-interest. She is a major strategic ally to the U.S. Israel is not a client-state, but a very reliable friend. To weaken Israel is to destabilize the region and risk the peace of the world, for the road to world peace runs through the Middle East.

God deals with nations in accordance with how those nations deal with Israel. Israel does not have to offer an excuse for its existence; Israel lives today as a right that has been hallowed by the Bible, by history, by sacrifice, by prayer, by the yearnings of the Jewish people for peace.

It seems the tyrants of this world must always have a scapegoat; someone, some ethnic people to blame for their own inequities. All too often, those people have been the Jews. Iranian leaders join Supreme Leader Ali Khamenei in castigating Israel as a puppet regime planted in the Middle East by Western Zionists simply to usurp Muslim claims to the land. Khamenei once again threw down the gauntlet when he asked:

> What are you? A forged government and a false nation. They gather wicked people from all over the world and made something called the Israeli nation. Is that a nation? Those [Jews] who went to Israel were malevolent, evil, greedy thieves, and murderers.[72]

Both of Iran's most visible leaders have further characterized Israel, at varying times, as a filthy germ, a cancerous tumor, a stinking corpse, and a "stain of disgrace [on the] garment of Islam." The intent is to demonize the Jewish people and label them a tool of the devil, a "manifestation of Satan"[73] to be used against the poor, unsuspecting Muslim people; to make the Jewish people seem subhuman—thus the moniker "monkeys and apes" often ascribed to Jews.

In my interview with Prime Minister Netanyahu, he alluded to Iran's determination to destroy Israel:

> Israel could be in great jeopardy; so will everybody else. In short order, the Western-oriented regimes of the Middle East would fall by the wayside. That is why you see the Arab countries siding against Iran, against Hezbollah; they understand what I am saying. The Middle East could be taken over, and that means the oil fields—the oil spigot of the world—would be in Iranian hands.[74]

He further stated:

> Imagine what would happen later if Iran were to have missiles that would reach into every European capital. Within a decade into the Eastern coast of the U.S., and would be armed not with explosives, but with nuclear weapons.

> Iran could inspire the 200 million...300 million Shi'ites....
> That's what it intends to do—inspire them into a religious
> war, first against other Muslims, then against Israel and the
> West. The reason they despise us so much, the reason they
> want to eradicate us is that they don't hate you because of
> us, they hate us because of you. They say we are the "Small
> Satan" and that America is the "Great Satan."[75]

Iran is obviously the greatest immediate threat to the state of Israel, as it is Iranian currency which funds many of the major terrorist movements determined to decimate the Jewish people and wrest their homeland from them. When the fundamentalism which fuels the likes of former President Ahmadinejad is married to the proliferation of its nuclear program, the threat to Israel grows exponentially.

What Ahmadinejad and the clerics who rule Iran appeared to overlook was that Israel possesses the capacity to retaliate on a large scale. It boasts an advanced anti-missile system in collaboration with the U.S., and has the capability of crippling Iran's growing nuclear program. "Israel has a whole arsenal of capabilities to make sure the Iranians don't achieve their result," said Efraim Halevy, former head of Mossad.[76]

Following the death of Ayatollah Ruhollah Khomeini, it seemed that the mullahs and ayatollahs in Iran were simply waiting for the likes of a Mahmoud Ahmadinejad to burst upon the scene, to verbalize their hateful rhetoric. Today it doesn't take much insight to determine the identity of those out to destroy Israel, or in other words to "wipe Israel off the map." What, I wonder, does the world really think of them? Are most people aware of this blind devotion to the Mahdi? Do most understand the mindset of ardent *Twelvers*, dedicated disciples of the Twelfth Imam? Their dedication will cause them to do anything to ensure that the world is made ready for the second coming of their messiah—even if it requires manufacturing an apocalyptic event to provoke a rush to Armageddon.

Unfortunately, one need look no further than Ahmadinejad's speech at the United Nations on September 17, 2005. He closed with the words: "O mighty Lord, I pray to you to hasten the emergence of your last repository, the promised one, that perfect and pure human being, the one that will fill this world with justice and peace."[77] No, he was not speaking of the return of Jesus Christ, but the coming of the Mahdi. Ahmadinejad went home to Tehran and regaled his compatriots with a story about how mesmerized his listeners were when he spoke:

> On the last day when I was speaking, one person in our group told me that when I started to say "*bismullah Muhammad*" he saw a green light come from around me, and I was placed inside this aura...I felt it myself. I felt that the atmosphere suddenly changed and for those twenty-seven to twenty-eight minutes, all the leaders of the world did not blink. When I say they didn't move an eyelid, I am not exaggerating. They were looking as if a hand were holding them there, and had just opened their eyes.[78]

The miniature martinet that led Iran had the audacity to write a letter to President George W. Bush and one to the American people. If I were to put the message of each into a nutshell, they were both basically saying, "Become Muslim and we shall all live at peace."

The intentions of Iran's leaders are deadly serious; they can neither be taken for granted nor underestimated. They seek converts to their fanatical lifestyle from every nation, not just among the Arabs. Remember after all, Iranians are not Arabs, but Persians. Theirs is not a racial war, but a religious one. Ahmadinejad revered terrorists, whom he defined as "martyrs": "Is there an art that is more beautiful, more divine, more eternal than the art of the martyr's death?"[79] He, and those like him, want nothing more than that every knee on earth should bow to the Mahdi, and believe there will be no real peace in the world until the whole world is Muslim.

It is belief in the Mahdi that drives the *Twelvers*. They are by far the largest group of Shias, making up around 80% of the total. *Twelvers* represent the majority of Muslims not only in Iran, but in Iraq and Bahrain. They also make up large communities in Lebanon, Syria and Saudi Arabia.[80] They believe the return of this descendant of Mohammad will come in a mushroom cloud suspended over Israel and America. The Mahdi's regime is a suicidal one, and reminiscent of the statement made by Ayatollah Ruhollah Khomeini:

> "I say let Iran go up in smoke, provided Islam emerges triumphant in the rest of the world."

Given the determination to usher in the Mahdi, it is likely that Iran's government will, with Ayatollah Ali Khamenei's blessing, continue its defiance against the Western world and forge ahead with Iran's nuclear program. According to Israel's Prime Minister Netanyahu, Iran is the greatest threat to Israel since that nation was founded in 1948. This is so true not only regarding the Islamic republic's atomic aspirations, but because Iran fully undergirds the fanatical groups that surround Israel—Hezbollah in Lebanon and Hamas in Gaza. Both groups have drawn Israel into wars to defend her citizens. Netanyahu has not ruled out a military strike against Iran's nuclear sites, and after several meetings with President Obama, the prime minister continued to reiterate that Israel reserves the right to defend herself.

Iran seems intent on standing aloof from the world community. Its leaders ridicule and zealously reject calls from the UN Security Council to halt the enrichment of uranium in the quest of nuclear arms. And yet, this same entity entrusted with peacekeeping has failed to recognize the link between Iran's pursuit of weapons of mass destruction and its persistent threats to Israel and the United States. The Security Council has become the proverbial ostrich that buries its head in the sand in order not to see the approaching threat to global safety. Its refusal to recognize the danger has made the United Nations an even more ineffective body. The leaders in Iran flaunt their violation of international law; thus far, no one has been courageous enough to challenge them. No one has made a move to hold them accountable—neither for their infractions in the nuclear arena nor for their terrorist activities.

The pursuit of nuclear arms has placed the Sunni states in the Gulf region on alert. Leaders are concerned about the vulnerability of their countries should Iran complete the fuel cycle and actually manufacture nuclear weapons. Iran, a Shia majority, would then possess the means to intimidate its moderate Sunni Arab neighbors and create a climate of fear throughout the Middle East. The ghost of a nuclear arms race between the more radical Shia and the moderate Sunnis hovers over the area and fuels anxieties. This is another obvious reason why an atomic Iran is unacceptable; it will precipitate a trillion-dollar arms race in the Gulf region and provide a nuclear umbrella for any terrorist state.

Given the hatred for Israel and the West demonstrated by the radical Muslim world, and Iran's fanatical pursuit of nuclear weapons, the question must again be asked: How can the West be saved? What will checkmate Iran's end-game in the nuclear arena? Will sanctions drive the country into bankruptcy? Will it be pressure from the U.S., the EU, Russia or China? Will globalization be the straw that breaks the backs of Iranian leaders? Will an embargo on refined oil be the answer? Will it be a direct strike on their nuclear facilities by Israel?

Many think erroneously that Iran has only one target—Israel—but nothing could be further from the truth. Stronger action needs to be taken to educate the global community as to the threat which Iran poses to civilization—to worldwide stability and wellbeing. Iran has long been described as simply a threat to the Jewish state of Israel and to the United States; that is a complete fallacy. The possession of nuclear arms by a fanatical entity, whether Iran, North Korea, al-Qaeda or any of the myriad other radical countries or groups, is a menace of great magnitude, and must be addressed with equal alacrity.

One of the avenues which must be explored is that of what the Western allies might be willing to discuss with Russia and China in order to gain their backing on the Iran question. The U.S. has negotiated with China on separate issues involving currency and Iran; what would be the end result should those become joint discussions?

China and Russia have formed what might be loosely described as a protectorate for Iran. This tripartite back-burner agreement has proven to be reciprocally advantageous for all. Steve Schippert, co-founder of the Center for Threat Awareness, says:

No nation at the UN Security Council has been more steadfast or consistent in resistance to U.S. and Western sanctions efforts there than either the bear or the dragon. The reasons for this are quite simple: Synergistic strategic advancement against a common enemy, oil and money. Iran is rightly portrayed as one of the most pressing threats to the United States and her interests. But Iran remains in many respects a piece on the chessboard of a greater Russian and Chinese game. Iran seeks greater power and regional domi-nance and enjoys the support of both Russia and China in its pursuits. Both afford Iran the protection of cover and interference at the UN Security Council and other diplo-matic endeavors, allowing Iran to continue its nuclear efforts under a fairly comfortable security blanket.

For Russia...the gains are monetary and psychological, with Iran as a major arms client...China...signed a massive long-term energy deal with Iran worth billions. The United States in particular had made...public calls for other nations to specifically stop making energy agreements until Iran complies [with UN calls for halting the nuclear program]. Signing the energy deal...[afforded] the oil-starved dragon energy relief... . All seek to weaken the United States to the point where each is enabled to act on their respective interests.[81]

Each of the three nations has a different agenda in seeking relationship with the others in the group: Iran wishes to gain superiority in the Persian Gulf and continue its support for the terrorist groups which act as its proxies; Russia, the once proud bear desires to regain a once-dominant role on the world stage; and China, the Johnny-come-lately to the international politi-cal scene wants to wrest the "superpower" title from the United States, and desperately needs the oil flowing in from Iran. So long as America remains strong politically, economically and militarily, those wishes will be thwarted. The United States needs to delineate ways to put increased pressure on both

Russia and China to bring Iran to heel and force the leaders of the rogue nation to the bargaining table.

Having taken a snake into one's bosom, it is imperative not to think all is well and relax one's vigil. It might behoove both China and Russia to take notice of an event which took place following the botched elections in Tehran in June 2009. According to a *Miami Herald* report:

> In Tehran University's huge prayer hall, the Islamic regime's most powerful clerics deliver heated Friday sermons to thousands. These diatribes are normally accompanied by the chant ``Death to America!"
>
> But at the last Friday prayers [July 17, 2009]—an electrifying event that will affect the core of President Obama's foreign policy—the loudest chants were ``Death to Russia!" and ``Death to China!" Also, ``Azadeh!" which means ``freedom" in Farsi... Consider the impact of this new list of enemies. Ahmadinejad has been trying to distract attention from rigged elections by blaming the West for stirring up demonstrations.[82]

The next issue to be addressed when contemplating the question of how the West can be saved from an apocalyptic event orchestrated by Iran is that of globalization. What is it and what effect might it have on saving the West from Iran's nuclear pursuits and apocalyptic mission? Globalization is defined as:

> A process of interaction and integration among the people, companies, and governments of different nations, a process driven by international trade and investment and aided by information technology. This process has effects on the environment, on culture, on political systems, on economic development and prosperity, and on human physical well-being in societies around the world.[83]

Globalization knows no borders, it crosses international boundaries. That is why the fight against terrorism in any form must first be global. No one is exempt from the hatred and fanaticism which grips radical Islamic countries such as Iran. Having explored the dangers of nuclear weapons in the hands of leaders such as those in power in Tehran, we must define ways in which the world community can halt the forward progress of an atomic Iran.

A unified world marketplace would have a major impact on the economy of Iran. Such global tools as the Internet, Twitter, Facebook, and etc., are used by terrorist groups to plot and plan strikes, to fundraise, and to engage new members; those same tools could be used to discourage trade with Iran. Globalization could be a vital tool in halting the forward march toward an apocalypse, but only if all world leaders are engaged. It directly affects markets, economies, communications, transportation, trade, service industries, and capital. It clearly could be a determining factor in whether or not sanctions against Iran were effective. It could be used to leverage Iran's oil-based economy.

In a speech delivered at the National Defense College graduation ceremony in July 2009, Benjamin Netanyahu addressed the effectiveness of globalization:

> Eventually radical Islam will be defeated by the global information revolution, by the freedom of ideas which are breaking out, through technology and through ideas of freedom. This won't happen immediately, but it will happen... The only thing that can postpone and disrupt the rate of the extinguishing of radical Islam is the possibility that it will be armed with a nuclear weapon.[84]

Another action that would require a global response centers on the credit card industry. The director of the Israel Atomic Energy Commission told me one of the greatest weapons the world has against Iran's nuclear program is the credit card. If the credit cards and bank accounts used by mullahs and members of the Revolutionary Guard were frozen, it would have an enormous and immediate impact on their nuclear ambitions. This would amount to tens of billions of dollars.

While there are those who feel that "globalization" is a word not to be used in polite company or in political circles, it might well be a most effective weapon against Khamenei and Iran's mullahs, if wielded unilaterally. It would require a united front which would of necessity include China and Russia, not to mention a decline in the purchase of crude from the Iranian oil wells.

Is oil a possible key to halting an atomic Iran? In 2008, an analysis of Iranian oil industry began:

> The Iranian oil and gas industry approaches its 100th anniversary bloated, corrupt, and nearly bankrupt, managing four times the employees but two thirds of the oil production it had before the Islamic Revolution of 1978-79.[85]

Even with that gloomy report, Iran continues to export 2.1 million barrels of oil per day. The majority of its exports go to Asia with Europe taking the leftovers. Japan is the largest consumer of Iranian oil with China a close second. While it is able to export crude oil, Iran is forced to import 40 percent of its refined petroleum because of increased demands which its refineries are unable to meet. Iran is, however, spending its oil and gas revenues to fund terrorism. Some estimates indicate that Hezbollah receives as much as $200 million annually from Tehran.

It is conceivable that Iran could be persuaded to halt its nuclear program if stronger sanctions against imported refined gasoline were implemented. This is one proposal being investigated by American lawmakers. The 111th Congress introduced H.R. 2194: Iran Refined Petroleum Sanctions Act of 2009. In Section 3, Amendments to the Iran Sanctions Act of 1996, the following is found:

> PRODUCTION OF REFINED PETROLEUM RESOURCES-
> Except as provided in subsection (f), the President shall impose the sanctions described in section 6(b) (in addition

to any sanctions imposed under subparagraph (A)) if the President determines that a person has, with actual knowledge, on or after the date of the enactment of the Iran Refined Petroleum Sanctions Act of 2009, sold, leased, or provided to Iran any goods, services, technology, information, or support that would allow Iran to maintain or expand its domestic production of refined petroleum resources, including any assistance in refinery construction, modernization, or repair.

A similar tactic was considered and then rejected by the Bush (43) administration. It was decided that trying to enforce a refined petroleum embargo would present a dangerous and complex challenge. Both Russia and China would have to be induced to join such an effort. Iran could retaliate by halting exports and bringing traffic in the Strait of Hormuz to a standstill. That could prove to be a fiscal nightmare for an already susceptible world economy.

With H.R. 2194 on the table, Iran retaliated by announcing that it would end refined petrol imports. Seifollah Jashnsaz, Managing Director of National Iranian Oil Company, announced that Iran has planned the erection of nine refineries. He added that the country is currently constructing seven refineries. He indicated that the star in the refinery crown was "the biggest and most outstanding of all refineries being constructed in Iran and makes use of state-of-the-art technology...The said refinery, once fully operational, can produce 35 million liters of petrol on a daily basis. The production will not only satisfy Iran's demand for petrol but will also be sold at export markets."[86]

If Iran continues on its course of nuclear proliferation the U.S. government must quickly take the extreme measure of a complete oil embargo, not allowing fuel to be sold by Iran or refined petroleum to be delivered to the country. This would collapse the economy of the Islamic terror state.

These are all things that could work against Iran: sanctions, engaging Russia and China, globalization techniques, and a refined oil embargo. These are all tools that could be instrumental in intercepting the countdown to Armageddon and saving the West from an Iranian-induced apocalypse.

COUNTDOWN

9 ISRAEL

CHAPTER SIX
CONCEALED WEAPONS

The Holocaust left those Jews who survived not only yearning for a way to protect themselves from future assaults by anti-Semitic despots. From the concentration camps of Dachau, Auschwitz, and Bergen-Belsen and their vow of "Never again" emerged a nuclear weapons program that provided assurance of Israel's endurance. Since her early days of independence, the nation has actively pursued nuclear capability.

In 1949, a special unit of the IDF Science Corps, *Hemed Gimmel*, began a two-year geological survey to seek uranium reserves in the Negev. While far from finding massive deposits of the element, retrievable amounts were discovered. Consequently, Israel has been actively investigating the nuclear option from its earliest days.

By 1952, Israel had established the Israel Atomic energy Commission (IAEC) chaired by Ernst David Bergmann. Also heading the Ministry of Defense Research and Infrastructure Division renamed Machon 4, Bergmann distorted the line between *Hemed Gimmel* and the newly retitled organization. In 1953 Machon refined a method for separating uranium from the phosphate deposits in the Negev and improved upon the method for creating heavy water. Israel had then acquired the means to produce necessary nuclear materials.

In 1953, Shimon Peres was named as Minister of Defense, and as such oversaw Israel's nuclear program. Peres later said:

> From the outset, I resolved to keep my role entirely out of the public limelight. ... For this reason, my name was never included in any formal committee created in the area of atomic energy. That did not, however, prevent me from effectively running the entire program on behalf of Ben Gurion, nor did it impair in any way my authority. Ben Gurion trusted me. Professor Bergmann worked with me with no reservations. In time, I was able to win the trust and confidence of the other scientists, engineers and senior personnel engaged in the project.[87]

Peres petitioned the French government for design and construction capabilities. France was a nation more than happy to assist the Israelis, given the frigid atmosphere that gripped Western powers and the ensuing cold war. At first glance, such an expensive endeavor was deemed to be too much for the tiny nation already surrounded by enemies. However, Prime Minister David Ben-Gurion was up to the challenge. Such helpful assistance from the French was likely less state-approved and more conscience driven. Though opposed by President Charles de Gaulle, many in the country sought to eradicate the stigma left by Vichy France's cooperation with the Nazis during World War II. A compromise was finally reached: Construction work by the French on the Dimona site would be halted; private establishments would be allowed to meet contractual obligations.

A U.S. spy plane pilot in the skies over Israel in 1958 spotted a construction site near the small Negev town of Dimona. From the air, the locale contained an extensive perimeter fence, buildings, and roads to and from the site. Initially dubbed a "textile plant", the Israelis later changed its classification to "metallurgical research installation."[88] A Corona satellite provided better intelligence in late 1960. Near the end of the year, Central Intelligence Agency Director Allen Dulles informed then-President Dwight Eisenhower that Israel had a nuclear reactor and was on the way to completing construction of an atomic bomb.

Even as Israel and France negotiated, newly-inaugurated President John F. Kennedy pushed Ben-Gurion and later his successor, Levi Eshkol, to refrain from further nuclear construction. Some conspiracy theorists actually think that his untimely death was directly related to the demands from Kennedy's administration that inspectors not only be allowed access to a construction site near Dimona, but that if the site proved to be a nuclear facility, it be closed. This collision course had been fixed during the last days of the Eisenhower administration, as rumors surfaced that a top-secret structure had begun to rise from the middle of the Negev.

Shortly after Kennedy's inauguration in 1961, the dispute reached a fever pitch. Unlike another Democrat, Jimmy Carter, Kennedy was not fundamentally antagonistic; rather, he had a unique compassion for the Jewish people. Kennedy was pressed by his advisers — who presumed that Israel had no choice but to comply — to push for access to Dimona. In their zeal, Prime Minister Ben-Gurion was denied entry to the White House; instead, he and the president met at the Waldorf Astoria in New York City. Their talks were centered on the site in the Negev.

Although Israel has never acknowledged having access to nuclear weapons, neither has the likelihood been repudiated. Perhaps it is time the United States develops a similar tactic to that of its closest ally in the Middle East: Tone down the nuclear rhetoric. It was President Theodore Roosevelt who so famously said, "Speak softly and carry a big stick." Or, a page could be taken from Ben Franklin's *Poor Richard's Almanac* and an old Italian proverb: "You can catch more flies with honey than with vinegar."[89] All nuclear powers might try keeping the oratory and threats to a minimum. Israel has adopted that low-key method—one that is used only when absolutely necessary for preservation. Israel's attitude has gone so far as to not refer to the "Dimona" project; rather it was labeled "the big thing." An advisor to John F. Kennedy studiously described it as "the delicate matter."[90]

U.S. financial assistance for the fledgling nuclear program arrived in Israel via funds raised by Abraham Feinberg, a close friend to Chaim

Weizmann. Edward Teller, a Hungarian Jew and theoretical physicist who emigrated in the 1930s was engaged in the Manhattan Project—the project to develop the first atomic bomb. On trips to Israel in the mid-1960s, Teller unapologetically counseled the Israelis to develop a nuclear bomb. For whatever reason, the CIA failed to note the activity surrounding atomic research and development in Dimona. Teller didn't toss the CIA a bone of information—or contention—until after the Six-Day War when he revealed that Israel very likely was in possession of a nuclear device.

The CIA, of course, told President Lyndon Johnson, but determined that the information should be withheld from the Defense and State Departments. By the 1968 presidential election, Defense Secretary Clark Clifford and Secretary of State Dean Rusk were well-aware of Israel's pursuits and insisted that nuclear inspectors be allowed inside every site in Israel that had strategic weapons, and that any sales of Phantom fighter aircraft should be linked with compliance to those demands. Israeli Ambassador Yitzhak Rabin led the fight against those who insisted on that policy with Abe Feinberg and UN Ambassador Arthur Goldberg assisting him.

Washington Post writer, George Perkovich, stated that throughout its history as a supposedly nuclear power:

> Israel has never claimed to possess nuclear weapons and has never used them to enhance its prestige or browbeat its neighbors. For Israel, the bomb has never been something to brandish, never a shield behind which to hide while it annexes territory or undermines domestic or regional rivals—as was feared the bomb would be for Saddam Hussein's Iraq and, perhaps, Ayatollah Ali Khamenei's Iran. It is a shield against annihilation.[91]

On October 6, Yom Kippur, the Day of Atonement and holiest day of the Jewish year, the Arab Coalition, comprised of Egypt, Syria, and Jordan, struck Israel with a sneak attack in the hope of finally driving the Jews into the Mediterranean. Israel was tragically caught off-guard, as most of its citizenry were in synagogues, and its national radio was off the air. Because people were enjoying a restful day of reflection and prayer, Israel had no immediate response to the coordinated attacks. Israeli intelligence had not seen the assault coming, and the military was ill-prepared for war.

Prime Minister Golda Meir said of the onslaught of the enemy:

> The Egyptians could run to Egypt, the Syrians into Syria. The only place we could run was into the sea, and before we did that we might as well fight.[92] At the outset of hostilities, Egypt attacked across the Suez Canal. The battle raged for three days, and then the Egyptian army established entrenchments, which resulted in an impasse. On the northern border, Syria launched an offensive at the Golan Heights. The initial assault was successful but quickly lost momentum. By the third day of fighting, Israel had lost several thousand soldiers. More Israeli soldiers fell on that first day than in the entire Six-Day War of 1967: forty-nine planes were destroyed, along with one-third (more than five hundred) of her tank force, and a good chunk of the buffer lands were lost that had been gained in the Six-Day War. The Israelis seemed to be on the brink of total destruction again.

On the fourth day of the war, in an act of desperation, Prime Minister Golda Meir reportedly opened up three nuclear silos and pointed the missiles toward Egyptian and Syrian military headquarters near Cairo and Damascus.

In Washington, President Richard Nixon intervened in inter-cabinet squabbles between Kissinger and Schlesinger and lit a fire under those who were inundated by legislative lethargy. The president came straight to the point, announcing that Israel must not lose the war. He ordered that the deliveries of supplies, including aircraft, be sped up and that Israel be told it could freely expend all of its consumables: ammunition, spare parts, fuel, and so forth in the certain knowledge that these would be completely replenished by the United States without delay. Author Seymour M. Hersh wrote that earlier in his presidency, "Nixon made it clear he believed warfare was inevitable in the Middle East, a war that could spread and precipitate World

War III, with the United States and the Soviet Union squaring off against each other."[93] He was now staring down the barrel of that war.

Nixon's insistence that armaments be airlifted to Israel to ensure her victory was because the president assigned a great sense of exigency to the task. He said, "You get the stuff to Israel. Now. Now!"[94] White House aide Alexander Haig said of Nixon's focus on Israel:

> As soon as the scope and pattern of Israeli battle losses emerged, Nixon ordered that all destroyed equipment be made up out of U.S. stockpiles, using the very best weapons America possessed.... Whatever it takes, he told Kissinger ... save Israel. The president asked Kissinger for a precise accounting of Israel's military needs, and Kissinger proceeded to read aloud from an itemized list. "Double it," Nixon ordered. "Now get the hell out of here and get the job done."[95]

In a *Jerusalem Post* editorial, Nixon insider Leonard Garment was quoted as saying: "It was Nixon who did it. I was there. As [bureaucratic bickering between the State and Defense departments] was going back and forth, Nixon said, 'This is insane....' He just ordered Kissinger, 'Get your [behind] out of here and tell those people to move.'"[96]

Secretary of Defense Schlesinger suggested that the United States dispatch three transport planes loaded with war matériel in what became known as "Operation Nickel Grass." When he presented the proposal to the president, Nixon angrily sent the secretary to do his bidding. When Kissinger returned later to explain yet another delay in the president's orders being carried out, Nixon snapped that the delayed planes were to get off the runway immediately.

Every available American plane carried conventional arms to Israel. The resulting supply was larger than the Berlin airlift that had followed World War II, and it literally turned the tide of the war. Nixon's quick action saved Israel from almost certain extermination and the world from possible nuclear war. He had carried Kennedy's agreement to militarily support Israel to the next logical level — a full military alliance.

The Israel Defense Forces (IDF) launched a counteroffensive within the week and drove the Syrians to within twenty-five miles of Damascus. Trying to aid the Syrians, the Egyptian army went on the offensive, all to no avail. Israeli troops crossed the Suez Canal and encompassed the Egyptian Third Army. When the Soviets realized what was happening, they scrambled to further assist Egypt and Syria. The Soviet threat was so real Nixon feared direct conflict with the USSR and elevated all military personnel worldwide to DefCon III, meaning increased readiness that war was likely. However, a ceasefire was finally worked out between the United States and the USSR, adopted by all parties involved, and the Yom Kippur War was ended.

In 1976 it was whispered by the CIA that Israel was in possession of as many of twenty nuclear weapons. That number was thought to have increased to as many as two hundred hydrogen-type bombs.[97] Journalist Kenneth S. Brower wrote that the tiny nation could have as many as four hundred atomic weapons[98] that could be launched from any platform.[99] Given all the attention paid to nuclear pursuits, Israel has focused mainly on conventional weapons around which to base its military might—backing that with the Samson Option, a term applied by Prime Minister Ariel Sharon as a biblical reference to the story of Samson, a Hebrew judge who brought down the pillars of the Philistine god, Dagon. His final words in Judges 16:30 were:

> "Let me die with the Philistines!" Then he pushed with
> all his might, and down came the temple on the rulers and
> all the people in it. Thus he killed many more when he died
> than while he lived.

The strategy would, in an attack by nations determined to see another Holocaust against the Jewish people, be the last resort. When in 2006, U.S. Secretary of Defense nominee Robert Gates publicly acknowledged that Israel had atomic weapons, it was declared that any Israeli who discussed that matter was subject to "arrest, trial, and imprisonment." The country's news-readers, looking for new ways to discuss the topic resorted to terms such as

"doomsday weapons" and the "Samson Option."[100] Of course, Israel's reluc-
tance to confirm her weapons resources has been openly substantiated over
the years. Some Israeli leaders have publically acknowledged their country's nuclear capability: Biophysicist Ephraim Katzir in 1974; Israeli military
leader and politician Moshe Dayan in 1981; Prime Ministers Shimon Peres
in 1998, and Ehud Olmert in 2006.[101]

For sixty years, Israel has been pursuing nuclear capability and readying
retaliatory weapons—if needed. The Jewish people are determined that no
longer will they be sitting ducks for an anti-Semitic world to use as target
practice.

Among the nations openly maintaining atomic weapons arsenals, most
are bound by non-proliferation treaties or by assertion that they are dedicated to arms reduction. One method to achieve that goal is to further lower
the profile of weapons: Refuse to brandish them during times of emergency,
and decline all opportunities to display their availability. In other words,
Israeli forbearance would outweigh Iranian egos. The world would be more
secure with nuclear bombs relegated to the basement instead of prominently
displayed on the front porch or paraded behind goose-stepping soldiers.
This has worked well for Israel over more than four decades.

CHAPTER SEVEN

THE CANARY

American journalist Alvah Bessie once proffered the defining answer—
one which can be readily applied to the current political climate: "That's
what the cat said to the canary when he swallowed him—"'You'll be all
right.'"[102]

Since May 14, 1948, Israel has heard the same asinine answer to her
predicament of being surrounded by irate Arabs, "Just give up a little more
land, you'll be all right." Nothing could be further from the truth. As the
world-at-large continues to cover its eyes, the Jewish state continues to be
far from okay.

Events in the Middle East are rapidly moving toward total chaos. Eyes
worldwide are directed toward every country but the one that is most important—Israel. It has been called the "world's canary in the coal mine." You
know the story of how miners carried canaries into coal mines to detect
poisonous methane gas. It was one of the first early-warning systems. Over
decades, the phrase has taken on new meaning. Imprisoned in a cage and
deep in a coal mine, the canary was certainly not the master of its fate yet it
continued to chirp. The tiny creature remained uncompromisingly cheerful
as it faced daily danger.

The Jewish people who live in constant danger in Israel, too, face each
day without compromise. Whereas they could cower in fear in bunkers and

bomb shelters, they choose to meet each new day with courage and resolve. They choose to live as free men and women, undaunted by the enemies that plague them.

Each of the countries that surround Israel—Lebanon, Syria, Jordan, and Egypt—is in upheaval to some degree. The only matter on which all can agree is their hatred for Israel and the Jewish people. It is likely few in the region are aware that centuries ago ancient prophets took up quill and ink and wrote the names of these nations on the pages of time.

The prophet wrote in Ezekiel 38:5 that Libya (Put) would join forces with a Muslim coalition that would invade Israel. There is no further reference to Libya in the Bible beyond a mention in Daniel 11:43 that it would be under submission to the Antichrist during the Tribulation. It simply fades into antiquity.

Of Egypt Isaiah 192-4 (KJV) records:

> And I will set the Egyptians against the Egyptians: and they shall fight every one against his brother, and every one against his neighbour; city against city, and kingdom against kingdom. And the spirit of Egypt shall fail in the midst thereof; and I will destroy the counsel thereof: and they shall seek to the idols, and to the charmers, and to them that have familiar spirits, and to the wizards. And the Egyptians will I give over into the hand of a cruel lord; and a fierce king shall rule over them, saith the Lord, the Lord of hosts.

When the Bible speaks of Syria it is usually in the context of "Damascus," the capital city. Isaiah 17-1-3 tells us:

> "The burden of Damascus. Behold, Damascus is taken away from being a city, and it shall be a ruinous heap. The cities of Aroer are forsaken: they shall be for flocks, which shall lie down, and none shall make them afraid (because the area will be destroyed and deserted). The fortress also shall cease from Ephraim, and the kingdom from Damascus,

and the remnant of Syria: they shall be as the glory of the children of Israel, saith the LORD of hosts."

It would seem from those scriptures that the city/state will simply vanish in the End Times. As to when that will occur, we do not know.

There are many who believe Jordan will fall into the hands of the Muslim Brotherhood as did Egypt, under whose rule the land of the Pharaohs now lies. The motto of the fanatical Islamist organization is:

> "Allah is our objective; the Quran is our law; the Prophet is our leader; Jihad is our way; and death for the sake of Allah is the highest of our aspirations."[103]The Brotherhood's first significant rise to power was in 1936, in opposition to British rule in Egypt. In a strange way, the British under Churchill gave the Muslim organization the strong motivation which brought it to power. And that cycle of rule seems now to have come full circle, as the bitter fruit of fanatical Muslim activity once again threatens the very existence of Israel.

Demonstrations in Jordan in early 2011 prompted King Abdullah II to take immediate steps to implement reforms in an attempt to forestall further protests. Dissenters clashed with about 200 pro-government supporters in Amman in mid-February. The dissenters insisted on an end to the Jordan-Israel peace treaty and called for political reform. Jordanians have been hard hit by rising prices and joblessness among the younger population, both attributed to the global economy.

The Islamic Action Front (IAF), an offshoot of the Muslim Brotherhood, vows to continue demonstrations until it has achieved its goal: "constitutional and legal reforms." In a veiled reference to riots in Tunisia, Egypt, and Libya, a spokesman added, "Jordan is not an exception from the glorious Arab nation which is now struggling to ensure its place under the sun."[104] According to the prophet Zephaniah (2:8-11, KJV) the Day of the

Lord—during or near the Great Tribulation, the nations that surround Israel will be harshly judged:

> I have heard the reproach of Moab, and the revilings of the children of Ammon, whereby they have reproached my people, and magnified themselves against their border. There-fore as I live, saith the LORD of hosts, the God of Israel, Surely Moab shall be as Sodom, and the children of Ammon as Gomorrah, even the breeding of nettles, and saltpits, and a perpetual desolation: the residue of my people shall spoil them, and the remnant of my people shall possess them. This shall they have for their pride, because they have reproached and magnified themselves against the people of the LORD of hosts. The LORD will be terrible unto them: for he will famish all the gods of the earth; and men shall worship him, every one from his place, even all the isles of the heathen."

The prophet's vision includes a land of desolation reminiscent of Sodom and Gomorrah—a Dead Sea-like landscape lain waste.

Yet many refuse to see the biblical truths as they are written in Revelation: The Four Horsemen of the Apocalypse saddle up to herald the approach of Armageddon. And on the sidelines, the canary waits, muscles alert, heart beating rapidly, feathers aquiver. Is anyone paying attention to these skirmishes that signal the beginning of the end?

Sadly, the Liberal Left in America has drawn a line in the sand and stepped over to the other side—away from our long-time ally, Israel. President Barack Obama's one-world view has placed him squarely alongside the United Nations. He has cast his lot with those who would see Israel much like Jesus portrayed the traveler in the Parable of the Good Samaritan—stripped, bleeding, and impotent to defend herself. Many leaders, not only in the United States, but worldwide have befriended those who pass by on the other side and ignore the threat Israel faces.

Israel stands as a shining beacon in a sea of darkness, an island of sanity in a sea of madness, abandoned by her friends, but determined to defend those in her care. In preparation, this tiny nation has installed "Iron Dome" what has been called its most advanced version of an antimissile defense system. Another new system for intercepting anti-tank missiles, the "Trophy-Windbreaker" system was battle tested in early March 2011. It successfully intercepted an anti-tank missile launched from Gaza.

It appears that despite only one country in the Middle East—Saudi Arabia—actually calling for a strike against Iran's nuclear sites, Israel is the one making preparations for whatever is to come. With Iran courting Syria and Egypt and with its proxies, Hamas in Gaza and Hezbollah in Lebanon fully entrenched, it is only a matter of time until the canary flies the cage and leaves the hapless "miners" to face the consequences of their hateful actions.

Israel's leaders are well-aware that without the aid of the world's premier fighting force behind them, the odds are grim. The percentage is the same as that of one of its Old Testament heroes, Samson. After having met the seductive Delilah, he revealed that his long locks were the secret to his strength. Lulling him to sleep, Delilah called in her Philistine cohorts who clipped her lover's locks.

The once-mighty Samson was then bound and dragged away to Gaza where he was blinded. In time, he repented of his perfidy and as his hair grew, so did his strength. Asking to be led to the pillars that supported the temple of the Philistines, he braced himself between the uprights, and brought the structure down on its inhabitants—dying in the rubble.

Journalist Rafael Frankel wrote in 2012 that little has changed:

> Forty-five years after the Six Day War, the names have changed, but a remarkably similar scenario is unfolding. Once again, Israel is threatened by an enemy that is developing a military capability that poses an existential threat to the Jewish state. Once again, that enemy's leaders speak frequently of seeking Israel's destruction. Once again, Jerusalem is seeking assurances from Washington that the United States will not allow blatant aggression to stand. And once again, an American administration appears, publicly at least,

to be wavering on the commitments it made to Israel at the
very moment when the stakes are the highest.[105]

    Sadly, our current president has shown little more than disdain for Israel. Our ally has been treated like a Cinderella—ordered about and demeaned. Rather than looking to Israel, the canary in the coal mine, for insight, Mr. Obama has cozied up to Israel's foes. The U.S. is playing the harlot and crawling into bed with whomever offers the best deal. The payoff: black gold and the promise of continued greatness. Little does Mr. Obama realize that America is more akin to the Revelation church of Laodicea described as wretched, miserable, poor, blind, and naked. Mr. Obama is the emperor—the leader whose new raiment is about to leave him exposed for all to see.

    For Prime Minister Benjamin Netanyahu and his government, the issue may not be one of bowing to outside pressure, but in withstanding it, and doing what is right for the people of Israel. Choosing to sail on alone in a sea of hatred and revulsion would perhaps be the hardest choice of all. It would take courage, fortitude, wisdom, and leadership unknown to those who blithely excel in telling Israel what to do.

    We might ask ourselves if the actions of countries in the West—including the United States—are based on genuine antagonism toward Israel or is it another display of the haughty condescension by those too blind to understand that they are jeopardizing the lives of the population of an entire country?

    Do they not realize the world stands on the brink of destruction; that Armageddon lurks just around the corner? The President of the United States has the opportunity of a lifetime; the opportunity to stand as a champion of Israel. Yet, he has shown no propensity to do so. Instead, he has bowed to the kings of this world, invited terrorists to talk, and turned his back on the canary that would warn of impending peril. Will he choose to ignore the signs until it is too late?

    It is time for Mr. Obama to take an unpopular stand; it is time for him to take his position firmly beside our brothers and sisters in Israel. It is time for the American people to call for accountability from their elected officials, and to post a warning that the job of defender of the brave and free is up for grabs. Only those who are willing to stand with our staunchest ally in the Middle East need apply.

Mr. Netanyahu was very vocal about the delay in setting time limits on Iran's nuclear pursuits:

> "The world tells Israel 'wait, there's still time'. And I say, 'Wait for what? Wait until when?' Those in the international community who refuse to put red lines before Iran don't have a moral right to place a red light before Israel....If Iran knows that there is no deadline, what will it do? Exactly what it's doing. It's continuing, without any interference, towards obtaining nuclear weapons capability and from there, nuclear bombs....So far we can say with certainty that diplomacy and sanctions haven't worked. The sanctions have hurt the Iranian economy but they haven't stopped the Iranian nuclear program. That's a fact. And the fact is that every day that passes, Iran gets closer and closer to nuclear bombs."[106]

Meanwhile, Israel must make the decision to either bide her time until she has garnered the support of fickle world leaders or go it alone. If the United States is sincere about curbing an attack on Iran's nuclear facilities, it must draw Prime Minister Netanyahu's proverbial "red line" in the sand of the Middle East—one that should Iran cross, a military option will be utilized. If not, to resolve the challenge, Israel must once again turn to the people determined to be fully trustworthy—themselves.

COUNTDOWN

8 THE UNITED STATES OF AMERICA

CHAPTER EIGHT

ALTERATION OR ALTERCATION?

2011 Pew Research Center survey determined:

> In most predominantly Muslim countries there is widespread opposition to Iran acquiring nuclear weapons. Only in Pakistan does a majority (61%) support Iran's nuclear ambitions, although significant numbers of Palestinians (38%) and Lebanese (34%) back Iran's acquisition of a nuclear arsenal.[107]

The country most profoundly affected by the Iranian pursuit of nuclear capabilities, of course, is Israel. Barack Obama seems less than interested in the overwhelming sense of jeopardy this places on the Jewish nation. In an interview with the president before his 2013 trip to Jerusalem, journalist Jeffrey Goldberg asked what exactly was meant by the repeated statement, "All options are on the table." The president explained:

> It means a political component that involves isolating Iran; it means an economic component that involves unprecedented and crippling sanctions; it means a diplomatic component in which we have been able to strengthen the coalition that presents Iran with various options through the

P-5 plus 1 [the five permanent members of the UN Security
Council plus Germany] and ensures that the IAEA [Interna-
tional Atomic Energy Agency] is robust in evaluating Iran's
military program; and it includes a military component....

In addition to the profound threat that it poses to Israel, one of our
strongest allies in the world; in addition to the outrageous language that has
been directed toward Israel by the leaders of the Iranian government—if
Iran gets a nuclear weapon, this would run completely contrary to policies
of nonproliferation. The risks of an Iranian nuclear weapon falling into the
hands of terrorist organizations are profound. It is almost certain that other
players in the region would feel it necessary to get their own nuclear weapons. So now you have the prospect of a nuclear arms race in the most volatile
region in the world, one that is rife with unstable governments and sectarian
tensions. And it would also provide Iran the additional capability to sponsor
and protect its proxies in carrying out terrorist attacks, because they are less
fearful of retaliation.[108]

Obama's latest flip-flop as an "immovable friend of Israel" is a departure from his rhetoric following the 2009 inauguration. Then, the president
extended an olive branch to Iranian leaders with his offer of "unconditional"
talks. The included wording closely resembled that of Jimmy Carter when, in
his 1981 State of the Union address, he made an offer to Khomeini, the mad
mullah of Tehran: "We are prepared to work with the government of Iran to
develop a new and mutually beneficial relationship."[109] The latest, almost
identical offer to Iran's government came from international envoy Javier
Solana. In typical fashion Ahmadinejad responded not by decreasing but by
increasing the enrichment of uranium.

In an article for *The Wall Street Journal*, Bret Stephens offered this
observation:

For three years, the administration has deferred to European and U.N. diplomacy while seeking to build consen-
sus around the idea that a nuclear-armed Iran poses unacceptable risks to global security...*Today, the international*

community is less intent on stopping Tehran from getting the bomb than it is on stopping Washington from stopping Tehran.[110] (Emphasis is mine.)

As a lame duck president now in his second term in office, Obama seems more intent on negotiating with the sworn enemies of the United States, i.e., Ayatollah Ali Khamenei and his purveyors of terror, than with those who seek freedom in the Middle East. In December 2012, the president reportedly proposed a plan to the Iranians that the two sides hold face-to-face dialogue regarding Iran's nuclear program—without consulting or coordinating with Israel. The report also stated that the U.S. was likely to close the window on negotiations after four to five months if no progress had been made. The next move could then be a military option.[111]

At the same time the Obama administration was making an attempt to draw Iran to the negotiating table, North Korea launched a satellite-carrying missile. The latest move from Pyongyang is further proof that the rogue nation, with which the US is still technically at war, has the capability to deliver a nuclear device to the west coast of the U.S. Iranian armed forces deputy chief, Brigadier General Masoud Jazayeri was quick to acknowledge that Tehran "congratulates the people and the government [of North Korea] on the successful launching of the satellite-carrying rocket."[112] Despite reports that Iranian experts were in North Korea, Tehran was equally swift to deny any collusion with that country. If those statements prove to be valid, Iran could be closer than was thought to having access to a missile delivery system that could endanger the Middle East, Europe, and the United States.

Among the options for dealing with Iran are sanctions—which have had some limited effect on the economy there—and regime change, which is not the policy of the Obama administration. This was made patently obvious in 2009. President Obama had a legitimate chance to support change for good, but he turned a blind eye to the freedom-seekers who took to the streets of Tehran to protest Ahmadinajad's debatable presidential victory. He had the opportunity to respond vigorously in support of the Iranian people, but failed to do so, and his silence was most telling. As Iranians risked their lives, Obama took a neutral stance. Dante Alighieri said, "The hottest places in Hell are reserved for those who, in time of great moral crises, retained their neutrality."[113]

It seemed that President Obama was determined to remain aloof to the cries of the people of Iran in favor of doing nothing in what appeared to be an attempt to preserve the possibility of negotiating with the very man who holds the Iranian people under his thumb—Ayatollah Ali Khamenei.

The young men and women of Iran who stood up to Ahmadinejad and had their votes stolen waited eight days before President Obama finally issued a statement. Even then, he offered no hope of any kind to the protestors. Did President Obama understand men and women weren't willing to die simply for a vote recount; but that they were willing to lay down their lives for the right to be heard, for the right to life, liberty, and the pursuit of freedom? They were not protesting faux ballots; they were protesting the despotic limitations imposed on them by the tyrannical clerics who really run the country.

The Islamic Republic in Iran was exposed as a fraud. If President Obama could not use diplomacy to support democracy, any hand he might extend to Iran's ruling mullahs had better have a whole lot of *baksheesh* (bribery money) in it.

According to Education Views website, Mr. Obama's reputation in Arab countries has suffered:

> Despite intense and sustained efforts to woo the Arab world with money and nice words, a newly-released survey of the region finds that President Obama is at the bottom of a list Arabs admire most. Obama is admired by just 4 percent of Middle East Arabs in the new survey released by Brookings Institution and University of Maryland. Above him:
>
> ✧ 13 percent preferred then-Iranian leader Mahmoud Ahmadinejad.
>
> ✧ 6 percent preferred dead Iraqi dictator Saddam Hussein.
>
> ✧ 5 percent chose the late Venezuelan strongman Hugo Chavez.

❖ Even 5 percent chose former French President
Nicolas Sarkozy over Obama.

And when asked if there could be just one superpower,
who would they like it to be, Arabs snubbed Obama again.
The top choice, with 22 percent, was China...the United
States came in at 7 percent.[114]

Should all of the administration's attempts to force an agreement from
the mullahs in Iran fail, the U.S. (and Israel) are left with just one response—
the military. There are a multitude of scenarios that could prove effective. For
the sake of brevity, only the minimum will be outlined here.

First: What steps might be taken in advance preparation for an attack?
The U.S. could position its aircraft carriers in strategic locations from which
they could steam toward the Arabian Sea and the Persian Gulf on a moment's
notice. Possibilities for combat duty would be Nimitz class carriers:

❖ *USS Ronald Reagan* (CVN 76) with Carrier Air Wing
One Four (CVW-14).

❖ *USS Abraham Lincoln* (CVN 72) with Carrier Strike
Group Nine and host to Carrier Air Wing Two.

❖ *USS John C. Stennis* (CVN 74) with an
embarked Air Wing (CVW-9) including eight
or nine squadrons consisting of Navy and
Marine F/A-18 Hornets, EA-6B Prowlers,
MH-60R, MH-60S, and E-2C Hawkeyes.

❖ The *USS Kitty Hawk* was decommissioned in
2009, but the *USS George H.W. Bush* could be
called into service in the Persian Gulf Region.

If the United States were to move two carrier task forces into the Persian
Gulf region, it would deliver a clear signal to Tehran of increased firepower
in the region available to launch a sea-based air strike.

The carriers would be supported by the U.S. underwater fleet that includes:

> The *USS Ohio* (SSGN 726), the first ballistic missile submarine to complete conversion to a new class of guided missile submarines (re-designated SSGN from SSBN). With guided missile capability, this new class of submarine is being reconfigured to support Special Forces capabilities on the ground. Three other submarines are undergoing the SSGN conversion process, including the *USS Michigan*, the *USS Florida*, and the *USS Georgia*. The U.S. Navy could deploy any of these attack subs to the Persian Gulf region to support Special Forces operations that might be involved in a strike on Iran.

Additionally, the U.S. Navy could announce any task force assignments that would deploy additional Tomahawk cruise missile resources in the Persian Gulf. Knowing that the U.S. Navy was deploying additional military resources to the region would clearly signal an attack on Iran.[115]

If the use of ground forces became necessary, there are several U.S. military bases that observers could watch closely for activity that might signal an attack on Iran.[116] Fort Rucker, Alabama, is where the Army has consolidated air support operations, including the Apache (AH-64A) attack helicopter, the Blackhawk (UH-60A) and the Kiowa (OH-58D) used in reconnaissance as well as target acquisition/designation missions.

The 16th Special Operations Wing (SOW) is stationed at Hulburt Field in Florida. That is the largest Air Force unit assigned to U.S. Special Operations Command, and is uniquely equipped to undertake missions in an enemy-controlled area or with politically sensitive objectives, such as Iran's nuclear facilities. Rather than launch a full-scale invasion of Iran, the unit could hit designated targets. Its motto is "Any Time, Any Place." The unit was responsible for the capture of Manuel Noriega in Panama and Operation Uphold Democracy in Haiti.

A third key base is Twenty-Nine Palms, the Marine Corps Air Ground

Combat Center near Palm Springs, California. It is located in a mountain-ous desert area that would be ideal for training in a physical terrain that resembles the sites of several key nuclear installations in Iran. Units from these three bases would be ideal to support a limited military incursion that could accompany a U.S. air strike on Iran.

We should also expect that the CIA director and the U.S. secretary of state might make trips to confer with NATO allies prior to any U.S. preemp-tive strike on Iran. The point is that before actually launching an attack, the ramp-up to any action could be used as an additional, final opportunity to increase pressure on the regime in Iran.

If the Security Council and the Obama administration are totally inef-fective in halting Iran's forward momentum in the nuclear race, the scenario would certainly shift to military preparedness.

It is expected that a reasonably short period will precede an attack, to issue a final ultimatum to Iran and to prepare the U.S. public for yet another preemptive war in the Middle East. Even in this final stage, when the U.S. military is positioning for attack, Iran still will have a last opportunity to realize the seriousness of the situation and recant. The probability of Iran reversing course after Security Council failures is small. If anything, Iran may become even more defiant.

As we have repeatedly noted, the religious zealots ruling Iran believe war and destruction are a necessary precondition for the second coming of the Mahdi. Moreover, the hard-liners in the Iranian regime judge that the United States will over-extend by attacking Iran, believing that Iran is destined to defeat the U.S. in a Middle East war. The Supreme Leader and his crew may see a war as the beginning of the fulfillment of Ayatollah Khomeini's predic-tion that Israel and the United States will fall, just as he had envisioned that the Shah, the Soviet Union, and Saddam Hussein would fall.

The U.S. attack on Iraq involved a military invasion with the inten-tion to move on Baghdad and depose the regime of Saddam Hussein. Let us assume, at least initially, that the U.S. strike on Iran would be more lim-ited, consisting primarily of an air attack combined with Special Forces Operations on the ground. A move to a full-scale invasion would only follow a U.S. acceptance that regime change was the official foreign policy with regard to Iran. The goal in a more limited military attack would be to knock out Iran's major nuclear facilities, causing a major setback in Iran's ability to manufacture nuclear weapons.

Should an attack become imminent, the following Iranian nuclear facilities would likely be primary targets: [117]

- ✧ Arak, the heavy water plant about 154 miles southwest of Tehran.

- ✧ Bushehr nuclear reactor, located along the Persian Gulf, approximately 250 miles south of Tehran.

- ✧ Isfahan nuclear processing plant.

- ✧ Natanz nuclear enrichment plant.

- ✧ Saghand uranium mine.

- ✧ Fordow uranium enrichment plant.

About a dozen smaller facilities devoted to Iran's nuclear efforts would also be targeted, some of which are imbedded within cities and will require precision bombing. While several hundred sites may play some role contributing to Iran's nuclear technologies, the goal would be to target the major facilities which would need to be destroyed to stop Iran's progress toward enriching uranium and pursuing nuclear weapons technology.

Iran's missile facilities have also been systematically catalogued and studied by U.S. military intelligence. Fairly comprehensive surveys are publicly available on the Internet. The National Threat Initiative (NTI), for instance, lists 29 Iranian missile production facilities by name, location, and function.[118]

Iran's military air bases, including army, navy, and air force are also well known to U.S. intelligence services; again, Internet resources make available many detailed descriptions of Iran's military forces and their base locations.[119] Iran's *Shahab* missiles are launched from mobile carriers; a satellite intelligence effort will have to be made in the days immediately prior to an attack to see if their current locations can be identified.

Secondary targets would be comprised of government buildings, including military facilities; Iran's media and telecommunications infrastructure, also radio and television stations; telephone switching facilities; government buildings; conventional power plants; bridges and highways; rail lines; port facilities.

Hardened structures, such as the underground centrifuge plants at Natanz, might be attacked with tactical nuclear weapons, either from ship-launched Tomahawk cruise missiles, or launched via air strike. Otherwise, the munitions utilized would be conventional, largely precision-guided bombs, such as those used in the 2003 attack on Iraq. Most likely, tactical nuclear weapons would not be employed, so as to keep the weapons threshold conventional only.

A more limited attack would see multiple waves of air strikes and cruise missile attacks. In a noted book about John Boyd, the fighter pilot whose ideas on air combat fundamentally changed the tactics of air warfare, author Robert Coram notes that air combat is a blood sport:

> Many civilians and those who have never looked through the gun sight—then called a pipper—at an enemy aircraft have a romantic perception, no doubt influenced by books and movies about World War I, that pilots are knights of the air, chivalrous men who salute their opponents before engaging in a fight that always is fair. They believe that elaborate rules of aerial courtesy prevail and that battle in the clear pure upper regions somehow is different, more glorified and rarefied, than battle in the mud. This is total nonsense. Aerial combat, according to those who have participated, is a basic and primitive form of battle that happens to take place in the air. Fighter pilots—that is, the ones who survive air combat—are not gentlemen; they are backstabbing assassins. They come out of the sun and attack an enemy when he is blind. They sneak up behind or underneath or "bounce" the enemy from above or flop into position on his tail—his six-o'clock position—and "tap" him before he knows they are there.[120]

Coram comments that effective aerial combat is a "knife in the dark." The same principle that makes one-on-one dog-fighting effective applies to massive air attacks. The goal is to exert enormous air power to destroy key targets as rapidly as possible; catching the enemy unprepared, even surprised, is most effective in what amounts to a modern application of Nazi Germany's World War II *blitzkrieg* tactic.

As with the "shock and awe" strike on Iraq in 2003, the attack could involve submarine and ship-launched Tomahawk cruise missiles, B-2 stealth bombers and F-117 stealth fighters, using precision-guided bombs and bunker busters.[121] This same type of massive airpower could be launched against Iran, with a focus on Iran's nuclear facilities and military bases.

CHAPTER NINE

CHANGING OR UNCHANGING?

If the goal in dealing with Iran is not regime-change, the plan would have to be altered. Attacks on the government infrastructure could be aimed at reducing its ability to communicate internally or organize an effective counter-attack. The air attack could occur over the span of a few days, with no plan to launch a ground invasion, unless Iranian counter-attack measures required an expanded war effort. While the air attack most likely would not eliminate Iran's ability to produce nuclear weapons permanently, the program could be significantly set back, perhaps to a point where recovery would be extremely costly, requiring several years to reach a pre-attack status.

Helicopter-delivered Special Operations assaults could supplement the air attacks by going after installations embedded in population areas or hardened targets that might be better destroyed by troops on the ground. The Special Operations strikes would most likely be defined as hit-and-destroy missions where there was no anticipation of a sustained campaign.

The overall design of such an offensive would be to inflict a hard blow over a limited time, with no expectation of launching a sustained invasion aimed at regime change. The goal would be to destroy as much of Iran's nuclear technology as possible, so we could set back any nuclear weapons program and gain more time to deal with the government in Tehran.

Inflicting major damage to Iran's nuclear facilities could be accomplished by the U.S. launching a blitz air attack. Unless Iran's military capabilities were destroyed in the first few hours, however, a counter-attack would be costly.

Many, if not the majority of the mobile *Shahab* missile launchers might survive air strikes, and be employed to hit select targets, including the many U.S. military bases in surrounding nations, including in Iraq, Kuwait, Qatar, Azerbaijan, and Oman. Thousands of U.S. military personnel could be killed in missile raids organized by Iran in the days and weeks following an air attack.

Additionally, Hezbollah terrorists in Lebanon as well as Hamas and the Islamic Jihad in Gaza would most likely launch retaliatory missile strikes on Israel. Iran, as well, could launch conventionally-armed *Shahab* missiles against Israel's major cities, with the likelihood of inflicting thousands of human casualties and causing substantial infrastructure damage.

If any Iranian military fighter planes survived, a missile war could be supplemented by Iranian fighter sorties against U.S. bases in the area and against Israel. Even a conventional missile war would cost thousands of lives on all sides and would almost certainly draw Israel into the conflict, even if the United States labeled the war a preemptive strike.

Within Iran today, there is a considerable base of opposition to the current regime, especially among Iran's youth and student populations. A tactical military strike launched by the United States against Iran risks backfiring. In reaction to the attack, the U.S. might stir up Iranian nationalism, even among the nation's dissidents. Following an attack, internal support for the Iranian regime might actually intensify. Iranians could oppose what would be portrayed as U.S. aggression against Iran, with the regime certainly arguing that the attack was completely unjustified.

If America were seen as opposing Islam, not simply going after Iran's nuclear facilities, a region-wide uprising might unify in support of Iran, regardless of whether the Muslims involved were Shiite or Sunni. Right now many of Iran's Muslim neighbors, including Turkey, are concerned about their own national security as Iran pursues nuclear technology aggressively. Even Saudi Arabia has taken a position opposing Iran's defiant pursuit of nuclear technology.

Following a U.S. strategic strike against Iran, many Islamic nations, including even Sunni Saudi Arabia, might reverse their policy, to express sympathy with Iran, if not offering outright support. By launching a pre-emptive attack against Iran, anti-American sentiment throughout the Islamic world could intensify.

Wherever terrorist sleeper cells have operational capabilities, a U.S. military attack against Iran would provide an occasion for renewed incidents. If the strikes were only limited to the type of rail transportation and subway bombs we saw in Spain and London, terrorists could cause havoc by launching raids in several Western countries simultaneously.

The U.S. would be blamed by those in the West predisposed to be sympathetic with Iran's argument that its nuclear program is for peaceful purposes only. As the world's only remaining superpower, the US would then be cast in the role of an international aggressor.

If the war against Iran were characterized as a war of self-defense, worldwide public opinion would most likely turn against the United States. A preemptive attack on Iran would bear heavy political consequences for the United States, not only in the Islamic world, but among many traditional allies as well. In the extreme, an attack against Iran could backfire, causing a rise of Islamic unity across the globe.

The aftermath of a military strike against Iran would be risky for the U.S., even if it achieved the objective of knocking out or slowing Iran's nuclear capabilities. A long war in Iran would be disastrous, given the potential to stir up anti-American terrorism and insurgencies in the aftermath. As we learned in Afghanistan and Iraq, a rapid military victory may only be the first chapter to managing a successful peace. Rather than stabilizing the Middle East, an attack on Iran might further destabilize the region, such that Israel's ultimate survival was even more at risk than before the attack.

Should the Palestinians unite behind Hamas and Islamic Jihad in reaction to a U.S. strike on Iran, it might well portend intensified political pressure against Israel for further concessions. In the extreme, the U.S. attack might occasion a new wave of terrorist attacks launched against Israel.

The following reasons, then, are an argument for the regime-change solution:

- ✦ If Ayatollah Khamenei remained in power
  after a U.S. preemptive military strike,
  a move toward declaring war on the
  United States might be the next step.

- ✦ The military strike might bring Iran's
  nuclear program to a halt, but that
  halt would only be temporary.

- ✦ The radical regime under the mullahs would move
  to reconstitute its nuclear program immediately.

- ✦ Moreover, those countries who feel the U.S.
  attack was unjustified might provide increased
  technical and financial support to Iran.

A U.S. military attack on Iran undoubtedly would cause world oil prices to spike. Oil would likely increase to well over $100 a barrel, pushing U.S. gasoline costs even higher. If the Iranian regime withstands a U.S. military preemptive attack, it would most certainly urge OPEC to restrict supplies. Approximately 40 percent of the world's oil supply passes through the Strait of Hormuz.

The decision to depose the current Iranian government would avoid leaving in place a regime that would declare the United States an enemy to be destroyed at all costs.

Once rebuilt, Iran's nuclear program would be harder to control. Having once defied the world community, Iran would not hesitate the second time to present the world with the choice of deposing the regime or facing the prospect of an atomic Iran armed with nuclear weapons. Having survived one attack, the Iranian regime might resolve to build a coalition of international allies into what could amount to a mutual security pact, where the allies declare that any further attacks will be considered an attack on Iran's allies.

Terrorist organizations would use the U.S. preemptive attack as the justification for their open declaration to obtain nuclear weapons and trigger a nuclear arms race in the region. Intensified terrorism in support of Iran would be aimed at further destabilizing the Middle East, Europe, and America.

The Iranian regime would have to rebuild the physical facilities destroyed in the attack. The human talent of Iran's nuclear scientists and engineers, however, would remain in place, unless a large percentage of Iran's nuclear experts were killed at facilities which the attack damaged or destroyed.

The second time the facilities are constructed would be easier than the first. Conceivably, better facilities would be reconstructed faster, cheaper, and be made more secure from future attack. Ironically, Iran's nuclear infrastructure might emerge superior to those destroyed.

In rebuilding its nuclear infrastructure, Iran could go immediately to advanced-generation nuclear technologies. Ironically, in the longer run, we might have done Iran a favor by eliminating old and experimental nuclear facilities, so the regime could rebuild its nuclear program with new, state-of-the-art technologies. Within a short time, Iran's nuclear program could be back, fully functioning, possibly even more advanced than it had been before the attack.

On January 16, 2006, Davoud Danesh-Jafari, Iran's economics minister, said that the country's role as the world's fourth-largest producer of oil gave Iran a position of power in the world oil economy. "Any possible sanctions from the west," he warned, "could possibly, by disturbing Iran's political and economic situation, raise oil prices beyond levels the West expects."[122]

This thinly-veiled threat of oil retaliation was intended to put the U.S., the EU, and the IAEA on notice. If this is Iran's response to possible Security Council review, how much more severe would the regime's response be to a military strike aimed at Iran's nuclear facilities?

A preemptive strike involves attacking the symptoms, not solving the problem. If this realization can be communicated to the political Left, especially to key Democratic Senators, and to the American people, an attack aimed at creating regime change in Iran offers a more realistic chance that the nuclear threat can be removed altogether, not just postponed.

Ironically, the political repercussions on the U.S. from a full-scale invasion of Iran might be less than would be realized from a more limited attack. With the Iranian regime left in place, the mullahs and their supporters would have a continuing podium from which to project their anti-American grievances.

Dissidents within Iran, as well as expatriate opponents of the regime worldwide, will have to come forward to reorganize what could hopefully emerge as a more democratic Iran. U.S. leaders would need to demonstrate a desire to withdraw once a new Iranian government had been installed. This is the same model the U.S. followed at the end of World War II, where the goal was to establish democratic governments in Germany and Japan, as a pre-condition for withdrawal.

The current regime in Iran is a central instigator of terrorism worldwide. As has been noted repeatedly, Hezbollah, Hamas, and the Islamic Jihad virtually owe their financial survival to the mullahs in Iran. Al Qaeda operatives work actively with the Iranian government to further mutually-held aims.

By eliminating the Iranian regime of the mullahs, a central part of the War on Terrorism would be won. Without support from the mullahs in Tehran, Syria would have a much more difficult time dominating Lebanon. Without constant discouragement from Tehran, the Palestinian Authority might have an easier time reaching a final agreement with Israel to implement a "two-state" solution.

The mullahs in Tehran have been a roadblock to Middle East peace since the 1979 revolution. As long as the current leaders remain in power, one cannot expect the War on Terrorism to end. With the regime of the mullahs gone, however, substantial sums from Iran's abundant oil profits would no longer be available to fund terrorism. With such interference removed, the War on Terrorism might make important strides towards reaching a successful conclusion.

Eliminating the regime of the mullahs would represent an important movement toward freedom and democracy in the Middle East, as well as provide the potential for a more complete reconciliation of Islamic peoples worldwide with the U.S. and other Western nations.

From this perspective, the United States might well calculate that rather than launch a limited strike on Iran's nuclear facilities, more would be gained by going after the regime itself.

Obviously, solving the Iranian nuclear crisis involves no easy choices. Rather, as I have noted, all options have negative consequences. The choice then is to find the best among admittedly undesirable choices.

Russia and China, while opposed to any U.S. invasion of Iran, would likely stand aside, having decided not to provide direct military assistance to save the regime of the mullahs. Skeptics worldwide will argue that an invasion of Iran would overstretch the U.S. military and prove too costly an undertaking. Yet, with U.S. military force levels having been reduced in Iraq and Afghanistan, redeployment to Iran is more achievable now. Clearly, a military invasion of Iran would not be the option first considered by any U.S. administration.

Yet, after a serious attempt is made to deal with the Iranian regime on a more limited basis of engagement, the Obama Administration may come to the conclusion that regime-change is the only option that truly makes sense. However, all other options should be explored first. Still, after months of pursuing more limited objectives and tactical methodologies, the fundamental choice may well be: remove the regime of the mullahs once and for all, or accept the reality that sooner or later the Iranians will end up with nuclear weapons.

If the mullahs wanted to be sure that no single country could deny access to the enriched uranium needed to run a peaceful program, then the IAEA could create a multi-nation "uranium bank" from which enriched uranium could be withdrawn. The Iranian nuclear crisis could be resolved fairly easily and quickly by mature and experienced international diplomats, provided that Iran's intentions are truly peaceful and that all defiance would cease. This includes attacking Israel with verbal threats and halting financial and war matériel support to terrorist organizations such as Hezbollah and Hamas.

In conclusion, the leaders in Iran have an easy solution to the entire crisis. If Iran's only intent with its nuclear program is peaceful as claimed, then all it has to do is comply with the IAEA's request for verifiable inspections.

CHAPTER TEN

I SPY!

here is one basic reality that cannot be denied: If the world community permits Iran to continue to enrich uranium, it is only a matter of time before the mullahs-in-charge have nuclear weapons. Every time one of the Western countries—be it the U.S. or a member of the European Union—mentions "unconditional negotiations" it is seen as a moral victory for Iran.

In 2006, Israel sent an Eros-B spy satellite into space.[123] It was, at that time, one of the most sophisticated available, and capable of spotting objects on the ground as small as 27 ½ inches (70 centimeters).[124] In the same year, Yitzhak Ben Yisrael, head of the Israeli space agency, gave an interview on his country's Reshet Bet Radio. He explained how the satellite would help Israel follow Iran's progress with uranium enrichment at Natanz:

> ...Even when you dig a tunnel to the depths, you see it in a photograph. You cannot know what is happening under the ground, but you can see where the location is, where it is, and even finer things, according to the dirt which is being taken out. You can even know how deep it runs. All kinds of things of this kind. [125]

Current satellite pictures confirm information collected at the tactical level, and top-quality resolution far outstrips earlier satellite data. Superior resolution makes the difference between simply seeing similar subjects and being able to determine specific war matériel on the ground. Is it a rocket launcher? A missile? What type? Is it an underground facility or simply the sunlight casting a long shadow on the ground? Such mundane objects as doors and windows can be determined on buildings. Not only can they be spotted; specific individuals can be identified. Iran's nuclear sites can be detected and ultimately targeted with the newer and more precise information.

In 2006, George W. Bush decreed that Iran must face penalties for its refusal to halt uranium enrichment. According to the then-president, "The world now faces a grave threat from the radical regime in Iran. The Iranian regime arms, funds, and advises Hezbollah."[126] The IAEA issued a rather redundant report (as in, "Haven't we heard that before?") indicating Iran had not suspended its uranium enrichment activities. This document opened the way for UN Security Council sanctions against Iran. With a new deadline in the offing, the mullahs had little left except more defiance and bravado.

U.S. ambassador to the United Nations John Bolton in August of that year signified he was in favor of levying more stringent sanctions straightaway, following the deadline. He indicated that the verbiage for the action would be in place before the target date. Bolton said, "In terms of what happens afterward, at that point, if they have not suspended all uranium enrichment activities, they will not be in compliance with the resolution. And at that point, the steps that the foreign ministers have agreed upon previously ... we would begin to talk about how to implement those steps."[127]

Although China, France, Russia, the United Kingdom and the United States (Security Council permanent members), along with Germany, offered an attractive incentive package to the tyrants of Tehran, Iran defiantly declined to cease nuclear activity. The inducements included membership in the World Trade Organization, help from the telecom industry, lifting restrictions on the importation of airline parts, and a "fresh start in negotiations."[128] Meanwhile, the Bush (43) administration averred that every possibility was still available and could be employed. This included the use of nuclear weapons—in an attack on Iran's nuclear facilities according to Seymour Hersh, an investigative reporter whose articles appear in various high-profile publications. [129]

Bush's successor, Barack Obama, changed both tactics and rhetoric regarding Iran. Before the Inauguration, he was interviewed on "Meet the Press" where he advised host Tom Brokaw that the U.S. should "ratchet up tough but direct diplomacy with Iran."[130] The president-elect added that in his opinion, it needed to be made clear to the Iranians that further nuclear development, backing of terrorists groups such as Hamas and Hezbollah, and attempts to intimidate Israel would not be acceptable.[131] Mr. Obama opined that the U.S. needed to make it abundantly clear that pressure needed to be applied to Iranian officials to halt the country's "illicit nuclear program."[132] After being sworn in as president, Obama gave one of his first television interviews to Al Arabiya, a Saudi Arabian-owned news channel. He was quoted as saying "if countries like Iran are willing to unclench their fist, they will find an extended hand from us."[133]

Unfortunately, Iran is not willing to 1) comply with IAEA policies and restrictions; 2) allow inspections of its nuclear facilities; 3) accept the presence of a Jewish state in the Middle East; and 4) "unclench its fist." This makes for an ongoing and very tense situation between the West and the fanatical Islamic state. It's quite easy to see that while U.S. allies have been busy wringing their collective hands, Iran has been linking hands with other fundamental Islamists in an ongoing effort to eventually bring down both "The Great Satan" and "The Little Satan."

After the IAEA met in late 2009, White House press Secretary Robert Gibbs suggested that Iran would pay if it continued to refuse to comply with IAEA demands. As opening of the Bushehr I plant neared in late 2010, Gibbs indicated that intelligence sources had discovered:

> "Russia is providing the fuel, and taking the fuel back out. It, quite clearly, I think, underscores that Iran does not need its own enrichment capability if its intentions, as it states, are for a peaceful nuclear program."[134]

In early 2012, Secretary of State Leon Panetta vacillated between

Iran not wanting to develop nuclear arms capabilities and already possessing them. By August, he had decided that the U.S. might have to resort to military alternatives in dealing with an Iran nearing nuclear capability. In so doing, he suggested, the U.S. might have to resort to armed intervention should negotiations fail.

Four months later, in January 2013, I.S.I.S., a think tank in the U.S. presented a paper stating that Iran would have the capacity to manufacture at least one nuclear bomb by mid-2014. The experts at the organization suggested that sanctions against the rogue nation should be tightened in order to restrict production. The document also suggested a harsher stance:

"The president should explicitly declare that he will use military force to destroy Iran's nuclear program if Iran takes additional decisive steps toward producing a bomb."[135] At this writing no such declaration has been forthcoming.

There is, however, one little-known advantage that the U.S. has over its ally, Israel—refueling tankers. Were Israel to undertake a lone attack against Iran's nuclear sites, a crucial role would be played by fuel tankers; Israel lacks a sufficient fleet. That shortage would place the Jewish state at a significant disadvantage. Israeli leaders are aware that the threat against the United States is not as dire as it is for Israel, especially with centrifuges and even new nuclear plants being added to operations in Iran almost weekly.

Perhaps the one advantage for Israel is in the area of credibility. It has already struck nuclear targets in Iraq and Syria. Warnings were not just empty words. Israel has proven its mettle; the Iranians know that.

Despite the rhetoric emerging from the hallowed halls of the White House, and Obama's insistence that Iran will not be allowed to secure a nuclear bomb, few take these words seriously. There are several reasons; one, the U.S. was involved in two major conflicts in the Middle East in a ten-year period. A third war could further weaken the economy—not only in the United States, but globally. And the question must be asked: Would allies support another Middle East war? Israel, on the other hand, is a known quantity with great credibility. If provoked, it will cross the "line in the sand" and go after Iran's nuclear facilities.

Were the U.S. to gift Israel with combat-ready refueling tankers, it would give Israel the advantage. It would also force Iran to take a step back—something some pontificators believe has already been done with the slowing of forward progress on the nuclear program. The Grand Ayatollah just might determine that the best course would be to call a permanent halt to the quest for an atomic bomb.

The only action that is likely to make the Israeli position more strategic would be increasing Israel's advantage with needed equipment. Will the U.S. respond appropriately?

Or, will it be that the prophetic words of British Prime Minister Winston Churchill ring once again across the mountains and plains of the "land of the free and home of the brave?" He challenged:

> "If you will not fight for right when you can easily win without bloodshed; if you will not fight when your victory will be sure and not too costly, you may come to the moment when you may have to fight with all the odds against you and only a precarious chance of survival."[136]

As the Western world watches events unfold and new questions arise on the nuclear stage, the Iranian people have elected their next president, Hassan Rowhani. That didn't work so well in the 2009 election when Ahmadinejad was reelected, not by the people, but crowned as continued leader by Ayatollah Khamenei. Resistance from the Green Party that had contested the reinstatement of the Tehran tyrant was met with murder, mayhem, and riots in the streets. With the help of his personal force, the Basij, Ahmadinejad retained the office and found himself at odds with the mullahs:

> Khamenei's main worry is not whether the opposition can regroup after being hammered following the post-election unrest in 2009....Instead, it appears Khamenei senses that the internal political rulebook could be under threat.

Ahmadinejad first broke taboos—and earned himself instant political

enemies—by challenging the authority of Khamenei in 2011 over the appoint-
ment of the powerful intelligence ministry post. Since then, Khamenei has
been gradually drawn into the mix despite the traditions of the Supreme
Leader remaining aloof from day-to-day affairs.

The unraveling of their relationship began when security forces crushed
the protests over Ahmadinejad's re-election. Ahmadinejad increasingly bris-
tled at having to take a back seat to the ruling clerics, who control all key
political and policy decisions.

A political temper tantrum in April 2011—when Ahmadinejad boycot-
ted meetings for 10 days to protest Khamenei's intelligence chief appoint-
ment—opened the flood gates. [137]

Many believe Khamenei has formulated a two-pronged tactic for the
2013 election: 1) He will maintain attempts to build momentum following
the March 2012 parliamentary voting; 2) He has to quash any infighting that
would derail his plan and risk losing his position of power. Khamenei is not
ignorant of Ahmadinejad's desire to have a puppet of his choosing win the
office of president. The Ayatollah's high-wire juggling act is a gamble—one
that tears away the safety net while leaving the Supreme Leader with his
hands full of political turmoil, a failing economy, and international sanctions
designed to bring Iran to its knees. Add to that the threat of an attack on its
nuclear sites by Israel and/or the United States and Khamenei is a train wreck
waiting to happen.

Do not be deceived: Even though Iran has a new president as of June 14,
2013, little has changed. Despite the label of "moderate", Hassan Rowhani
will wield only the power he is allowed to exercise. One thing that did not
surface before the election, at least not in the mainstream media, is that the
winning candidate was successful because he had been among those hand-
picked by the Supreme Leader. Rowhani was also endorsed by Ayatollah
Ali Akbar Hashemi-Rafsanjani, one of the staunchest supporters of using
nuclear weapons against Israel.

Rowhani, a moderate in its narrowest definition, is in actuality, an
extremist who wants to continue the nuclear program—not for peaceful purposes, but to destroy Israel. The difference between this latest president and

his predecessor is that Rowhani is more polished, shrewder and much more diplomatic. And, he has taken the first and major step to success: He has the Western media in his pocket.

COUNTDOWN

7 RUNS, HITS—NO ERRORS

CHAPTER ELEVEN
A SHAPE IN THE MOONLIGHT...[138]

In 1981 Israel launched a surgical strike against Iraq's *Osirak* reactor and excised the cancer lurking undercover in Saddam Hussein's front yard. It was an audacious, but effective, move by the Israeli Air Force (IAF) to thwart the demented dictator's attempts to secure a nuclear weapon.

"Operation Opera" was launched on June 7 of that year. The task force included fourteen F-15s and F-16s, which took off from Etzion Air Force base in the Negev. The pilots' route took them over Jordan and Saudi Arabia and into Iraqi airspace. Their mission was to attack and destroy *Osirak*, the nuclear reactor built for Saddam Hussein by the French.

While on vacation in Aqaba, Jordan's King Hussein is said to have seen the Israeli planes as they flew overhead. He attempted to notify the Iraqis, but it was apparent that his message either did not reach its destination, or the Iraqis chose to ignore it as speculation.[139]

Although the surprise attack shocked the Iraqis and the world, it had not been planned overnight. It was the final resort after all diplomatic efforts had failed and the French could not be persuaded by world opinion to halt construction of the reactor. Prime Minister Begin consulted closely with his Cabinet. A decision of monumental proportions was reached; the only avenue open to insure that Saddam Hussein did not achieve nuclear arms capabilities and thereby carry out his threats against Israel was to attack *Osirak*.

Intelligence sources within Israel determined that within one to two years, Iraq would have possessed nuclear weapons. Later resources confirmed that Saddam was, in fact, within one year of his goal.[140]

Prime Minister Begin and his Cabinet did not take lightly the choice to attack Hussein's pet project. Moshe Dayan, Begin's foreign minister, worked zealously through diplomatic channels to forestall such an attack. Casper Weinberger and Alexander Haig, defense secretary and secretary of state under Ronald Reagan, agreed with the Israeli evaluation of the seriousness of the circumstances in Iraq. However, the U.S. refused to take the lead in combating the situation. It might have been that the true danger was not evident, or simply that Iraq was engaged in a war with Iran, an avowed enemy. Had not the Grand Ayatollah Ruhollah Khomeini abandoned the Shah's nuclear program because it drew from the "Satanic" West, it is highly likely that he would have used any available nuclear weapons against Iraq. The same may be said for Hussein against Iran…or both against Israel, an avowed enemy of Islam.

Israeli Minister of Justice Moshe Nissim recorded that Prime Minister Begin was likely swayed to approve the attack because he realized that an unprincipled and irresponsible Arab ruler such as Saddam Hussein would not have thought twice about launching an attack on Israel. Begin realized the exigency to stop Hussein's quest for nuclear arms.

The Israelis explored every option open to them militarily—jets, ground troops, paratroopers, helicopters - before making the final decision to remove a fuel tank on each of their newly-purchased F-16s in order to make them capable of transporting the armament needed to destroy *Osirak*. More important, perhaps, was that they could make the foray, flying under Iraq's radar, without having to refuel. The date of the attack was set after Begin was notified that Iraq was about to take possession of a shipment of enriched uranium fuel rods from France. This was crucial because once the rods were in place the danger of nuclear fallout from the attack would have been a certainty.

Yitzhak Shamir stated the obvious in Israel's decision to act:

Deterrence was not attained by other countries—France and Italy—and even the United States. It was attained by the State of Israel and its Prime

Minster who decided, acted and created a fact that no one in the world today—with the exception of our enemies—regrets.[141]

The Israeli attack was relatively simple because Iraq had only one major nuclear facility. If Israel were to launch an attack on Iran's nuclear facilities today, it would be much more complicated and the consequences would likely be catastrophic in nature. The attempt may look much like the 2007 attack on the emerging Syrian reactor—undergirded by North Korea.

The East Asian nuclear power, long under the control of a family of dictators, has been known to sell atomic information to the highest bidder. Their most recently documented attempt lies at the bottom of a crater in the Syrian Desert. Located at a remote spot near the River Euphrates, it was covertly assembled with help from Democratic People's Republic of Korea specialists and supposedly unknown by IAEA watchdogs.

Unfortunately for Syria's President Bashar al Assad, the undercover facility was discovered by the Israelis and destroyed. It took only a matter of a few short days for the remains of the joint operation to be whisked out of sight, the area cleansed, and a new structure erected over the original spot. Non-nuclear proliferation countries may have been vexed to learn of North Korea's meddling, but exacted no penalties. It simply opened the door for other nuclear-seeking Middle East countries to look to the Korean Peninsula for the technology and equipment to build their own bombs. North Korea has certainly signaled its readiness to provide assistance.

In a speech in 2006, shortly after a North Korean nuclear test, then-President George W. Bush spoke of the incident:

> The North Korean regime remains one of the world's lead-ing proliferators of missile technology, including transfers to Iran and Syria. The transfer of nuclear weapons or material by North Korea to states or non-state entities would be con-sidered a grave threat to the United States, and we would hold North Korea fully accountable for the consequences of such action.[142]

The president reiterated:

This was confirmed this morning in conversations I had with leaders of China and South Korea, Russia and Japan. We reaffirmed our commitment to a nuclear-free Korean Peninsula. And all of us agreed that the proclaimed actions taken by North Korea are unacceptable and deserve an immediate response by the United Nations Security Council.[143]

The problem with such avowals is that when the nuclear site was discovered, neither Syria nor North Korea faced any significant after-effects from the Bush administration or other Western powers. Israel, the neighbor with the most to lose had to face and resolve the issue alone.

Innovative measures aren't always heralded on the front page of the *New York Times* or the *International Herald Tribune*. Such was the case when the Israeli Air Force struck a suspected nuclear site northwest of Damascus on September 6, 2007. In the aftermath of the attack, global attention focused on Syria's nuclear ambitions, but little was released about the actual incursion.

As information began to emerge, it was revealed that the attack was likely the first incidence of "electronic" combat—also called "non-kinetic"[144] warfare. The plan in such a move is to use electromagnetic transmissions to alter, destroy, or seize the opposition's military systems without initiating perceptible loss. It is, in essence, military computer hacking and electronic intelligence methods designed to reduce enemy capabilities. Israel discovered it was not only conceivable, but doable.

As the incursion was being made ready, an Israeli strike force slipped into Tall al-Abyad, Syria, a border town near Turkey. The group disabled two radar systems, enabling Israeli jets to overfly airspace without detection by the Syrian air force. That was a major coup, as Syrian radar defenses were considered the most complex and exhaustive in the Middle East.

The actual bombing run was carried out by ten Israeli F-15I *Ra'am* fighter jets attached to the Israeli Air Force 69th Squadron. The aircraft were armed with "laser-guided bombs, escorted by F-16I *Sufa* fighter jets and a few [electronic intelligence]... aircraft....Three of the F-15s were ordered back to base, while the remaining seven continued towards Syria."[145]

Following the attack, Ehud Olmert, Israeli Prime Minister contacted

Recep Tayyip Erdoğan, Turkish prime minister, to inform him of the circumstances. Erdoğan was then asked to forward a communique to Syria's Assad. The message in blunt form: "Don't try to build another nuclear plant." The Syrian dictator was urged not to make media fodder of the attack, and was assured the Israelis would show restraint as well.

CNN was the first to report the bombing; Olmert's comment was:

> "The security services and Israeli defense forces are demonstrating unusual courage. We naturally cannot always show the public our cards."[146]

Questions to Israeli sources regarding how the feat was accomplished were met with restrained silence. Perhaps it was a run-up to the time when such undetected incursions would mean a matter of life and death for the small Jewish nation, i.e., threats of being "wiped off the map" from the likes of Iranian leaders.

An attack scenario might read as follows:

> On a quiet Sunday morning in Israel, an observer glimpsed a shape passing briefly between earth and the moon. Its outline was that of a jumbo jet. It would be hours before the onlooker would know the truth: The attack on Iran's nuclear sites had begun. The first phase was not with bombers laden with rockets, but with an unmanned drone designed to scramble Iran's electric facilities, Internet, cell-phone, and emergency first-responder networks. The disruption to those facilities was being delivered via an unmanned airliner, possibly the *Eitan*.

While that scenario may seem far-fetched, according to the Homeland Security News Wire:

UPI reports that the 4.5-ton Heron TP, dubbed the *Eitan* (Hebrew for "strong"), is 79 feet long. It has a wingspan of 86 feet — about the size of a

Boeing 737 airliner — and stays aloft for 20 hours at high altitude, a capability Israeli UAVs have hitherto lacked.

Powered by a 1,200-horsepower turbojet engine, it has a maximum altitude of 40,000 feet and can carry hundreds of pounds of equipment, such as high-resolution cameras and electronic systems and presumably weapons.... The air force declines to specify what missions the *Eitan* will fly, or whether it was designed for use against Iran.... Elbit [Systems of Israel] recently announced the development of the Hermes 900, with longer endurance, higher ceiling and advanced satellite communications. It, too, is reported to be able to reach Iran.[147]

The *Eitan* can also be used as a detection device:

> The Israelis can detect preparations for missile launches in western Iran, 1,000 miles to the east, through an AN/TPY-2 X-band radar built by the U.S. Raytheon Co. deployed in 2009 at Nevatim Air Base in the Negev Desert south of Tel Aviv.[148]

The Israelis employing a UAV system designed to disrupt communications, radar, and computer systems could well be the first step in the countdown to an attack against Iran's nuclear facilities. It would not be out of the question for Israel to first use every means to prevent early warnings in Iran in order to launch a successful clandestine operation.

Another tactic that could be used to disrupt Iran's pursuit of a nuclear bomb would be to improve on the Stuxnet computer worm that attacked the internal workings of computers at one of Iran's nuclear plants.

In the summer of 2010 computers in Iran, India, and Indonesia were targeted by a sophisticated computer virus—Stuxnet. An article in *The New York Times* revealed a possible link with Stuxnet:

> The United States has never acknowledged its role in creating the Stuxnet virus, nor has it said anything about the huge covert program that created it, code-named Olympic Games, which was first revealed earlier this year by *The New York Times*. President Obama drastically expanded the

program as a way to buy time for sanctions to affect Iran, and to stave off a military attack on the Iranian facilities by Israel, which he feared could quickly escalate into a broader war.[149]

When researchers finally traced the malware, they discovered that the worm had been designed to attack something bigger than home computers; its target was thought to be one of Iran's nuclear sites—probably the nuclear reactor at Bushehr, surmised experts with Siemens software systems. Ralph Langner alleged the program was intended to "look for very specific Siemens settings...and then it injects its own code into that system....[the target] must be of extremely high value to the attacker."[150]

The nuclear plant at Bushehr did experience some delays and slow-downs after its system was infected by the Stuxnet worm. Fingers have been pointed at Israel and the United States; however, there are other signs that point to a Russian company also working on the site. While a credible target, Bushehr may not have been the only one. Other areas, i.e., refineries, factories, and chemical installations, would also be credible objects.

Langner believes the original computer worm is no longer a challenge:

> "Stuxnet is history. The problem is the next generation of malware that will follow."[151]

A new generation of the computer worm could provide needed disruption during the days and weeks before Israel makes the determination to bomb Iran's nuclear reactors.

CHAPTER TWELVE

TWENTY-FIRST CENTURY CYBER WORMS

In 2008, Israeli President Shimon Peres' first "Facing Tomorrow" Conference commemorating the sixtieth anniversary of the declaration of the state of Israel brought together some of the greatest minds in today's world to discuss what the future would look like for the global community, the Jewish people, and the nation of Israel.

Of the myriad of topics discussed at the conference, one I found particularly interesting concerned what the first wars of the twenty-first century would look like. The speakers believed they would come in four waves (and remember, this was in May of 2008):

> An economic attack: In a world where a growing number of corporations have more money than countries and hundreds of billions of dollars can be transferred in seconds, calling in loans or putting pressure on heavily-indebted nations could have the effect of a stealth bomb on a national economy. In states that are heavily corrupted, the ability to bribe and make contributions to re-election funds can put politicians into the pockets of unscrupulous corporate

moguls or wreak havoc on economies by manipulating their currencies or stock markets.

A cyber-war: With the incredible growth of the Internet as a source for news as well as virtually anything else you would like to know, media wars using the World Wide Web could turn the tide of opinion in a nation in mere hours. A battle for the hearts and minds of entire continents could be sparked through the focused attention of just a handful of people making posts and writing blogs. Social media quickly becomes a means of organizing protests or voicing opinions otherwise suppressed in a state-controlled media. Not only that, but through the use of viruses there is the potential to bring networks, power and communication grids, and entire industries to a grinding halt.

Proxy wars: War would be sublet to outside parties. As happened in Korea and Vietnam, larger, richer nations could fight each other through lesser states and organizations. However, now it is no longer about superpowers and who has the largest arsenal, but about who has the money, who would be willing to use their arsenals at any cost, and who could best manipulate their puppets to get them to do what they want.

Boots on the ground: The final wave would be a conventional invasion of armed forces marching in to take control as an occupying army. If the first three waves went well, then this one would be nothing more than a formality, with just a few skirmishes of local resistance rather than all-out battles between national armed forces.

The first three phases of such a war would be virtually invisible—a "spirit war" to manipulate individuals as if they were pawns. The idea would be to win their allegiance and participation through the speed of the Internet and work them up into frothing mobs that would take on tanks by their sheer numbers. As we have seen in the Middle East recently, such early phases would topple governments in days, and conventional fighting would only have to be a strategy of last resort.

The speakers at the conference stated that the more democratic and bureaucratic a nation, the more ineffective it would be in its responses to the waves of such invisible wars. Leaders would be paralyzed by media scrutiny as every step they took would be broadcast around the world the moment it occurred, accompanied by running commentary and criticism like some sort of sporting event. People would see things develop as they happened on their computers, smart phones, on network and cable news channels—or as they heard it on the radio, read articles and blogs, and read about it on their e-readers and tablet computers. Every action would be revealed immediately, and whether right or wrong, it would instantly be controversial.

Now fast-forward almost five years to where we are as I write these words. Look at what has happened in the world in the past half-decade:

> Hezbollah, an Iranian-funded proxy, was able to form a majority government in the Lebanese parliament. The new prime minister of Lebanon has been handpicked by the terrorist group—and Hezbollah is still the prime suspect for the assassination of Lebanon's last prime minister. Hamas has effectively done the same thing in Gaza, joining with the Palestinian Authority in hopes of forming a national government with it in Gaza and the West Bank.

WikiLeaks was able to obtain top-secret documents and communications from the United States and its embassies. Then it began systematically releasing these sensitive documents over the Internet, giving the U.S. diplomatic corps around the world a serious black eye, revealing sensitive information about U.S. strategies and potential actions, and exposing the corruption and lack of integrity of the governments that were home to these diplomats.

Many suspect it was Israeli intelligence that temporarily derailed Iran's nuclear program twice—setting it back potentially years—not with an air strike but by using a computer virus. According to one official I spoke with, the Stuxnet worm that was loaded into the computers at Iran's Natanz facility was "more lethal than an ICBM. A direct [missile] hit on a centrifuge would not have done as much damage as this virus had done." The attack shut down from 5,000 to 6,000 of the estimated 10,000 centrifuges at Natanz, severely crippling Iran's ability to enrich plutonium to weapons-grade. Some speculate that Iran could have a nuclear device within months, others believe the earliest Iran will be able to produce a nuclear bomb is 2015. Experts have been amazed at the speed with which Iran has replaced the damaged P-1 centrifuges.

These are all examples of the three waves of war that will precede a "boots-on-the-ground" invasion of another nation. With these options available, it seems obvious that Israel would launch any air strikes against Iran's nuclear sites with a well-designed plan to scramble its communications facilities.

Symantec is one of two major computer virus companies to closely study the use of cyber-attacks as a military weapon. As part of the analytical process, the Stuxnet attack in Iran as well as banks accused of laundering funds transferred from Iran to its proxy, Hezbollah, were closely scrutinized. The second company, Kaspersky Lab, released its finding regarding the Flame malware that also targeted servers:

> The Flame malware, including all of its components, was very large and our ongoing investigation revealed more and more details since that time. The news about this threat peaked on 4th June 2012, when Microsoft released an out-of-band patch to block three fraudulent digital certificates used by Flame. On the same day, we confirmed the existence of this in Flame and published our technical analysis of this sophisticated attack. This new side of Flame was so advanced that only the world's top cryptographers could be able to implement it.... we definitively confirmed that Flame developers communicated with the Stuxnet development team, which was another convincing fact that Flame was developed with nation-state backing.[152]

Identification of the Flame virus was the latest in a sequence of interrelated cyber-attacks that targeted Iran's computer systems since mid-2010—Stuxnet, Duqu, Flame, and Gauss..

A malware expert at Kaspersky Lab revealed:

"It is not the sort of cyberweapon you see developed by criminals looking to access bank accounts nor is it the sort of weapon used by activists to make a political point. Those often use very available tools to write the programs....only the attackers can read it through strong public key cryptography. These features are not normally found in malware created by everyday cybercriminals, reaffirming our initial conclusion that Flame is a nation-state sponsored attack... Flame was massive and complex and we have identified the nicknames of at least four individuals involved in developing it."[153]

Even with the discovery of these cyberworms, it is unlikely they are the latest, most effective to be launched by covert programmers. Was Israel involved as some suspect? Was the United States fishing for information with Stuxnet and other computer worms? The answers, of course, have not been heralded across the banners of Liberal Left newspapers. But there is no reason to believe that nations will not use every means available to protect against an Iranian nuclear attack. Should Israel choose this type of covert action before an attack against Iran, it seems there are a number of options available.

6 THE SHADOW OF WAR

CHAPTER THIRTEEN

LEAVING ON A JET PLANE...

Were Israel to launch an electro-magnetic or non-kinetic attack against Iran, *Eitan* drone(s) would soon be called into action. That would be joined by Israel's top Special Forces brigade unit 262, the equivalent of the SAS, and the F-15I strategic 69th squadron. These bombers are thought to have the capability of striking Iran and returning to Israel without refueling. (Potential targets of an Israeli air strike are approximately 950 to 1400 miles from Israel.)

In as little as three hours after the *Eitan's* departure, the skies over Israel would be filled with airplanes on a secret mission to destroy Iran's nuclear facilities. At Ramon Airbase southwest of Beersheba, seventy-five F15I and F16I aircraft would be launched in waves of twenty-five. During that time, it is thought that Israel would have fired over 5,000 air-launch weapons, including 500 BLU-109 and BLU-113 bunker buster bombs. Communications and radar inside Iran would already have been jammed, and it is likely that Israel would have launched at least one plane equipped with the IAI/Elta EL/M-2075 Phalcon airborne early warning system, very plausibly with additional command and control options.

Also in the air would be the B61-11, a nuclear-armed version of the BLU-113 to destroy the Natanz reactors, as well as target the uranium processing plant at Isfahan, the Russian-built reactor at Bushehr, and Saghand,

Iran's uranium mine. Should Israel have to face Iran alone, it would employ both air and ground forces against several nuclear targets in the hopes of stalling Iran's nuclear program for years.

In April 2005, Israel purchased one hundred GBU-28 bunker buster bombs (or hard target penetrators) and the WGU-36A/B guidance control unit and support equipment. The package was thought to be valued at $30 million.[154] The GBU-28 is touted as one of the deadliest of conventional weapons, and was a mainstay in the invasion of Iraq in 2003. The bombs would be deployed from Israel's F-15 planes. In 2006, Israel requested that the weapons be delivered sooner than scheduled: Fifty-five GBU-28's were delivered to Israel in 2009.[155] Ordnance for each bomb is a 5,000 pound conventional weapon with a 4,400 pound warhead containing 630 pounds of high explosives.

The weapon is capable of penetrating 20 feet of reinforced concrete or 100 feet of earth. The GBU-28 was designed after the 1991 Gulf War began, to penetrate hardened Iraqi command centers located deep underground.[156] The bunker buster bombs will fit on the F-15 and F-16 fighter aircraft the U.S. had previously sold to Israel. The weapons would serve well in attacking the underground nuclear facilities the IAEA knows Iran had built to harden nuclear installations from air attack.

Israel's larger nuclear warheads have been adapted for the *Jericho* series of missiles. Israel first began developing these missiles with French assistance in the 1960s. The *Jericho II* is a solid fuel, two-stage missile that Israel has test fired into the Mediterranean Sea at ranges estimated at around 1,300 kilometers (800 miles). Reportedly, Israel has a multi-stage *Jericho III*:

> It is estimated that the *Jericho III* entered service by 2008.
> The *Jericho III* is believed to have a three-stage solid pro-
> pellant and a payload of 1,000 to 1,300 kg. It is possible
> for the missile to be equipped with a single 750 kg nuclear
> warhead or two or three low yield MIRV warheads. It has an
> estimated launch weight of 30,000 kg and a length of 15.5
> m with a width of 1.56 m. It likely is similar to an upgraded
> Shavit space launch vehicle. It probably has longer first and

second-stage motors. It is estimated that it has a range of 4,800 to 11,500 km (2,982 to 7,180 miles), and probably significantly greater with a smaller payload of 350 kg (the size of one smaller Israeli nuclear warhead). It is believed that the Jericho [III] is inertia-guided with a radar-guided warhead and silo-based with mobile vehicle and railcar capabilities.

According to an official report which was submitted to the American congress in 2004, it may be that with a payload of 1,000 kg the Jericho [III] gives Israel nuclear strike capabilities within the entire Middle East, Africa, Europe, [and] Asia...[157]

Israel also has cruise missiles which can be adapted with nuclear warheads, such as the *Popeye Turbo* which is designed to be air-launched from Israel's F-15 and F-16 fighter jets.[158] The newest fighters in Israel's attack force are the Lockheed-Martin manufactured F-16I Soufa ("Storm") fighters. The second mainstay of the IAF is the 1990s Boeing-built (originally McDonnell Douglas) F-15I Ra'am ("Eagle") fighter planes. Both aircraft have a strike radius that should extend to targets in Iran without having to be refueled. But the distances involved would not leave much, if any, room for error.

The F-16Is are fitted with a pair of removable conformal fuel tanks that can be mounted on both sides of the upper fuselage, to hold 450 gallons of extra fuel, plus detachable wing tanks carrying another 600 gallons of fuel.[159] The F-15Is carry 4.5 tons of fuel in the internal tanks, conformal tanks, and detachable tanks, giving the F-15I an unprecedented range of 4,450 kilometers (2,765 miles).[160] Still, a mission without refueling would be pushing the performance window of the aircraft.

Information provided by a European policy group, Equilibri, speculates that an Israeli assault against Iran would include: "20 F-15s, 20 F-16s, 22-26 F15 C/Ds and F-16-Ds, 7 tanker KC-707/135s, and 2 Dolphin class-submarines to enter the Gulf of Oman.[161]

Should the decision be made for an attack against Iran's nuclear sites, it would be much more complex than previous surprise assaults. The Israelis have proven to be exceptionally imaginative and resourceful, and of necessity play their cards very close to the vest. There are, however, key questions needing to be asked and resolved.

The first issue would be the route from Israel to Iran. There are at least three choices from which to map an ingress and egress:

> Israel could choose a northern route. IAF jets would follow a trajectory that would take pilots north over the Mediterranean Sea toward Turkey. The flight path would then lead the jet planes east along the border between that nation and Syria and then along the Iraqi border into Iran.

The southern option would place Israeli jets in the airspace patrolled by the Saudi Arabians. While it seems unlikely such a move would be welcomed, the Saudis are so concerned about Iran's Shi'ite motives, it could produce "Operation Blind Eye," a scenario where the IAF would simply be ignored as it makes its way into Iran.

The most likely scenario would be simply for Israel to fly over Iraq. Since the U.S. military has withdrawn, Iraqi leaders are less capable of patrolling their own air space. That alone would allow the Israelis to make an incursion into Iran.

According to *Foreign Policy* writer Dr. Scott Firsing:

> Iran has in its possession Russia's S-300 Russian ground-to-air radar systems. The S-300 is considered one of the world's most versatile radar-missile systems and can simultaneously track hundreds of semi-stealth cruise missiles, long-range missiles and aircraft, including airborne monitoring jets. According to military sources, as many as ten intruders can be simultaneously engaged....
>
> Israel recently teamed up with Greece, who also has the S-300, to obtain information on how to defeat Iran's radar system. Israel flew a number of its jets into the S-300's massive electronics and was able to record details about defeating,

jamming and circumventing the potent radar system. The exercise was appropriately called "Glorious Spartan."

Israel itself has the assistance of NATO's early warning radar station in Turkey, which is there to protect the Jewish State against Iranian missile attacks. Ankara agreed to host the radar in September [2011] as part of NATO's missile defense system aimed at countering ballistic missile threats from neighboring Iran.[162]

The second issue would be the range IAF jets would have to fly to reach their targets and then return safely to Israel. While a round-trip flight of such distance might be possible given the optimum route, it could present problems if a longer route were necessary. With limited in-air refueling options, Israel would have to find an alternative—a temporary facility in the desert or landing on a U.S. carrier.

Fortunately, Israelis are masterful at making provision for survival. There is little reason to think they would launch any kind of covert action without first having counted, and recounted, the cost and their options.

National Security Analyst Anthony Cordesman believes, "They [Israel] will probably only get one strike [at Iran]."[163]

The bottom line is that Israel could destroy Iran's most important nuclear facilities by launching a massive air strike designed to last a few days at most. If Iran retaliated substantially, Israel could expand the attack with tactical nuclear weapons, suggesting Israel's willingness to escalate the conflict if necessary.

As the countdown continues with the launch of an air attack, what role might Israel's fleet of submarines play in such an attack? An offensive led by sea-launched cruise missiles would save Israel's fighter jets for later sorties. Such an onslaught could target major facilities, such as Isfahan and Natanz, as well as Iran's reactor at Bushehr and its heavy-water facility at Arak, where major damage could be inflicted before any fighter plane had to enter Iranian air space.

COUNTDOWN

 **DOWN TO THE SEA IN SHIPS**

CHAPTER FOURTEEN

HEL YAM—THE SEA CORPS

The Israel Navy is not an entity unto itself; it is attached to the IDF, but with more self-sufficiency than the other branches of the Israeli Defense Force. Formally known as the Sea Corps (*Hel Yam*), its commander enjoys the position of senior advisor to the chief of staff and bears a two-star rank. Even so, it is the smallest of all the Israeli military units with some 9,500 active sailors and approximately 10,000 reservists available should the need arise.

Compared to other nations, the Sea Corps is neither renowned nor sizeable, but like every other aspect of the tiny state on the Mediterranean, it is effective. The more thrilling endeavors of the Israeli air and land forces have long dominated the news, but that does not diminish the role of the navy in helping keep Israelis safe.

The story of the Israel Navy actually began in 1948 during the War of Independence. From its inception, the fleet ruled the seas in the region and proved its superiority by sinking the jewel of the Egyptian naval fleet—the *Emir Farouk*. In the years following, the Sea Corps added vessels, gunboats, electronics, and radar. Sailors were trained and the IDF added another layer of protection for the Jewish people in the State of Israel.

As yet another war threatened the nation the Sea Corps again exhibited its prowess by salvaging a Russian MIG, used widely by the Egyptian Air

Force. The operation gave the Israel Air Force a rare opportunity to scavenge the aircraft and study its systems and vulnerabilities. Added to that feat was the capture of the *Ibrahim al-Awal* in October 1956. It was a splendid opportunity for the IDF; the tanker was taken to the Port of Haifa where it was reequipped, renamed the INS *Haifa* and launched as the navy's third destroyer.

During the Six Day War in 1967, the Sea Corps used what was then outdated and outmoded naval equipment to patrol Israel's coastline along the shores of the Mediterranean. The navy captured Sharm-el-Sheik on the Sinai Peninsula and added another nearly five hundred miles of shoreline to patrol and protect. Following the war, the Israel Navy suffered two catastrophic losses—the INS *Eilat,* a destroyer, was sunk, and several months later, a submarine, the INS *Dakar* was lost during its maiden voyage from Portsmouth England to Israel. The sunken vessel was not discovered until thirty-two years later:

> On 24 May 1999 a joint U.S.–Israeli search team using information received from U.S. intelligence sources and led by subcontractor Thomas Kent Dettweiler of the American Nauticos Corporation, detected a large body on the seabed between Crete and Cyprus, at a depth of some 3,000 meters (9,800 ft). On 28 May the first video pictures were taken by the remote operated vehicle *REMORA II*, making it clear that *Dakar* had been found. She rests on her keel, bow to the northwest. Her conning tower was snapped off and fallen over the side. The stern of the submarine, with the propellers and dive planes, broke off aft of the engine room and rests beside the main hull.[164]

In 2000 part of the submarine was finally freed from its watery grave:

> On Wednesday, October 10 of that year the Nauticos team and the Israel Navy began to raise the conning tower to the surface. After nine hours of work, the tower was finally

raised at 4:30 a.m. to symbolically finish her voyage to the
Haifa naval base. The Nauticos expedition leader, Detweiler,
said: "To be the first to stand on the bridge of the *Dakar* after
32 years, attaching lines to secure her to the deck of our ship
for the final leg in the voyage home to Haifa, is a feeling I
will remember forever. She rode into Haifa standing upright
and proud, the Israeli flag flying over her. These images will
be with me for eternity." The conning tower was taken to
Haifa and today it stands outside the Clandestine Immigra-
tion and Naval Museum, remaining a poignant monument to
Ra'anan and his crew who remain on eternal patrol.[165]

It would be the Yom Kippur War in 1973 that would prove the Israel
Navy's readiness for combat following the sinking of a number of Egyptian
vessels with no losses among the Sea Corps, and "it was the first naval battle in
history to see actual missile combat conducted and electronic warfare deception measures taken."[166] The battles along the shores of the Mediterranean
were fierce and effective:

> The Battle of Latakia,... took place on October 7, 1973,
> the second day of the war. Five Israeli missile boats had been
> heading towards the Syrian port of Latakia, and sank a Syrian
> torpedo boat and minesweeper before encountering five Syr-
> ian missile boats. The Israelis used electronic countermea-
> sures and chaff rockets to evade Syrian missiles, then sank
> all five Syrian missile boats. This revolutionary engagement,
> the first between missile boats using surface-to-surface mis-
> siles, proved the potency of small, fast missile boats...The
> battle also established the Israeli Navy,...as a formidable and
> effective force in its own right.

The second naval battle which ended in a decisive Israeli victory was the
Battle of Baltim, which took place on October 8–9 off the coast of Baltim and
Damietta. Six Israeli missile boats heading towards Port Said encountered

four Egyptian missile boats coming from Alexandria. In an engagement last-
ing about forty minutes, the Israelis evaded Egyptian Styx missiles using
electronic countermeasures and sank three of the Egyptian missile boats with
Gabriel missiles and gunfire. The Battles of Latakia and Baltim "drastically
changed the operational situation at sea to Israeli advantage".[167]

By 1988, the Egyptian navy was two times larger than Israel's Sea Corps,
but was far outclassed in both technology and defensive dominance.

The vigilance of the Israel Navy is of paramount importance, given
that the boats patrol two distinct and disconnected bodies of water—the
Mediterranean and Red Seas—and employs a choice band of highly trained
and effective underwater military assault personnel. This group has proven
to be victorious in a number of operations.

The U.S. Sixth Fleet has been assigned to patrol the Mediterranean Sea.
With that task has come a cordial relationship between American sailors and
the Israel Navy. The Port of Haifa frequently welcomes the sailors as U.S.
ships are resupplied and undergo repairs. Because of strong ties between the
two allies, various joint maneuvers and naval exercises have been conducted
by the groups in such areas as shoreline strategies, anti-submarine warfare,
and various drills to test the readiness of the Israel Navy and the Sixth Fleet.

Despite its size, the Sea Corps has been tasked with maintaining peace
and security along Israel's shorelines. Because of that important job, most of
the naval fleet is dispatched from the ports of Haifa and Ashdod, with a few
vessels in the Red Sea—mostly the Dabur-class inshore patrol boats.

With more recent purchases from Germany, Israel has established a presence undersea as well as sailing the waters of the seas that meet the beaches
of the country. The Israel Sea Corps—the Hel Yam, born from desperation
and fueled by determination has become well-known for its compact, yet
commanding, presence and is well capable of fending off any adversary that
would attempt an assault by sea.

CHAPTER FIFTEEN

A SEA OF TROUBLES[168]

Just as Israel is the nuclear powerhouse in the Middle East, so she is seeking to become the same in the realm of the sea. In May 2012, the fourth of six Dolphin Class submarines ordered from Germany was added to the Israel Navy. This state-of-the-art boat will be of enormous help in keeping track of enemies, protecting the latest gas discovery off-shore in the Mediterranean, and to bolstering the blockade of the Gaza Strip—an attempt to halt the importation of illegal arms to one of Iran's proxies. And, with a price of more than $500 million, it is Israel's most expensive addition.

The Dolphin Class subs—which are believed to be fitted with nuclear weapons—also provide Israel with a second-strike capability designed to discourage surprise enemy offensives. To further develop its retaliatory response, Israel plans to have ten submarines in its fleet.

According to Defense Minister Ehud Barak, the subs are a much-needed infusion "in the face of growing regional challenges."[169] Barak also recognized the potential of the Dolphin class boats should an attack on Iran be unavoidable.

A senior officer in charge, Capt. Sassi Hodeda, responsible for the development of electronic combat systems said in an interview with Gulfnews.com:

> The submarine is a very important vessel, both in times
> of peace and of war. They have many uses. During peace

they are used for intelligence gathering and during war they become attack vessels. They can be used offensively to attack someone who is thinking about doing something stupid... [He added:] The sea is very important and we are doing as much as we need to keep the seas open....There are a lot of capabilities I'd like to have: to improve our ability to use radar at sea, to learn more about and use USVs [unmanned surface vehicles].[170]

USVs could become a very important tool in Israel's arsenal. They could be used not only for patrolling the new gas production platforms, but to stealthily approach unidentified vessels and secure information. They could also be used to engage enemy ships in times of war.

The US is considering the purchase of USVs in preparation for a clash with Iran in the Persian Gulf—whether that comes in 2013 or later. It is possible that the US navy will purchase the unmanned boats equipped with robotics. Why is that important? Information gleaned from intelligence sources indicate that Iran is building a fleet of suicide bomb boats for use in the event of an attack by Israel and/or the U.S. According to intel, the boats will be manned by Revolutionary Guard officers.[171] The fleet would be used much like the craft that bombed the USS Cole in Yemen in 2000—and the Japanese kamikaze attacks during World War II.

According to foreign reports, Israel's Navy has recently started using the robotic boats and has armed them with anti-armor "Spike" missiles.

The U.S. Navy has fired missiles from several unmanned surface vehicles (USV) in tests which took place off the coast of Maryland. All six test-firings were reportedly accurate.

"The tests are a significant step forward in weaponizing surface unmanned combat capability," Mark Moses, the U.S. Navy's drone boats program manager, told Wired Magazine.

"The boats could be used for a number of applications, including harbor security, and in various defensive operations and scenarios, which are of primary concern for the Navy," Moses added.[172]

To safeguard its seamen, according to Offiziere, a Swiss website:

Israel began experimenting with industry-owned Protectors [a robotics kit] in 2006. Today the IDF says Protectors are "operational," but will neither specify how many of the robots it possesses, nor describe in detail the [robots'] tactics. But it's clear the Protectors play a role in screening potential suicide boats before sailors board them. Israel's Protectors can be fitted with the same family of Typhoon remotely-operated, stabilized weapons mount that now equips many of the navy's most modern patrol boats, including the Super Dvora and Shaldag classes. Typhoon, built by Rafael, can be fitted with a wide range of guns, plus Rafael's Spike ER guided missiles, alongside radar or infrared and electro-optical cameras for targeting. The addition of Spike missiles to the Typhoon mounts was a response to the *Hanit* attack, Eshel said. Typhoon, firing Spike missiles, gives patrol boats greater stand-off range against shore targets — reportedly up to five miles.[173]

Sources also relate that the patrol boats outfitted with Protectors can be used in major combat situations.

The Israel Navy currently consists of the aforementioned nuclear submarines, in conjunction with three *Sa'ar* 5-class corvettes, the largest surface warships in Israel's naval fleet. The ships carry a crew of 71-74 and are comparable in weapons and swiftness to a frigate (similar to a destroyer escort vessel.) The Sa'ar 5 is outfitted with "sonar, torpedoes, missile launchers, electronic warfare capabilities and decoys, a gun mount, and a helipad and helicopter hangar."[174]

Experts believe that both the IDF navy and air force are equipped to launch low-yield tactical nuclear weapons, and would do so were Israel threatened with an attack. The capability also exists to propel *Jericho II* missiles with nuclear warheads skyward should Israel bomb Iran's nuclear sites.

According to Leo Rennert with *American Thinker*:

The bottom line is that nobody knows for sure if nuclear

deterrence would work again. This is why preventing Iran from becoming a nuclear power is the pre-eminent moral imperative of our age. An exchange of nuclear attacks would be a global catastrophe affecting all of mankind.

In the meantime, Israel is prepared for any and all existential threats—acting where feasible in concert with the international community but, if necessary, on its own. Its growing Dolphin fleet is a timely reminder of what's at stake. Containment might not work the second time around.[175]

CHAPTER SIXTEEN

COMPARATIVELY SPEAKING

On April 21, 2013, U.S. Secretary of Defense Chuck Hagel made his first trip to Israel as part of President Barack Obama's cabinet. As he launched his week-long visit, Hagel was quick to assure the Israeli public "Israel will make the decision that Israel must make to protect itself, to defend itself."[176]

One of the Defense Secretary's agenda items during his visit was to attempt to conclude an important arms sale between the U.S. and Israel. The transaction includes: V-22 Osprey transport helicopters, KC-135 refueling aircraft, advanced radar and other equipment. This sale would strengthen an already robust Israeli Defense Force, by far the most vigorous in the region.[177] The Israeli military is also set to receive $3.1 billion in aid in 2013; the largest infusion yet for any U.S. ally.

Iran, of course, will not sit idly by and allow an attack to go unanswered. But just how capable is the Iranian military, and how would it fare in an all-out clash with Israel? Detractors are eager to point out that Iran has Israel outnumbered in active and reserve military personnel. While that's true with approximately 750,000 IDF troops compared to Iran's almost 1.2 million, the truth is that Israel's troops—both active and reserve—are a well-trained, professional unit. Iran's reservists are much less so, relying more on brutality and less on disciplined response.

In addition, Iran ranks far below Israel not only in military matériel, but also in the condition of those armaments. In February 2013, Iran boasted of a new fighter jet, the Qaher-313, and its technology. Can the West really trust those amazing revelations? As one writer opined:

> Iran often holds military drills and announces weapons advances that it says are for purely deterrent purposes, though some analysts are skeptical of such reported advances because they cannot be independently verified.[178]

What of the naysayers who declare unabashedly that Israel would face certain ruin in an attack against Iran? Some of the loudest cynics come from the United States. In separate analyses regarding Israel's ability to successfully curtail Iran's nuclear program, *The New York Times* and the German newspaper, *Die Welt* took opposing positions in opinion pieces in February 2012. *The Times* was very skeptical of Israel's chances while Hans Rühle, a former head of the German Defense Ministry during the 1980s was confident of Israel's competence and prowess. Rühle fully believes Israel could strike a blow to Iran's nuclear program that would set it back ten years or more.

While the German is convinced that Israel's only hindrance is a shortage of refueling its fighter jets, the *Times* author surmised that it would require at least 100 IDF jets to accomplish the task that was called a Hurculean challenge. Michael V. Hayden, former CIA director (2006-2008) avered that such an attack was "beyond the capacity"[179] of the IDF.

> Another "ray of sunshine", U.S. Lt. Gen. David A. Deptula, reported, "All the pundits who talk about 'Oh, yeah, bomb Iran,' it ain't going to be that easy."[180]

In an acute juxtaposition to Deptula and Hayden, Rühle firmly disagreed with the pomposity of the two "experts." He carefully analyzed the Israeli Air Force arsenal, and what he felt to be the number of bombs required to eradicate Iran's nuclear threat. His conclusion was that Israel was more than capable of causing serious damage to the fanatical nation's nuclear program.

David P. Goldman, of the popular PJ Media website, has written: "Hans Rühle was one of the toughest and most perspicacious analysts in those heady days"[181] throughout the Cold war. Goldman also believes, "Rühle is highly confident that Israel could knock out Iran's nuclear program for a decade or more with about 25 of its 87 F-15 fighter-bombers and a smaller number of its F-16s. Each of the F-15s would carry two of the GBU-28 bunker busters, with the F-16s armed with smaller bombs."[182]

Some experts agree that satellite surveillance is solid and has given Israel good intelligence information should an attack become a necessity. Rühle in particular thinks the GBU-28 bunker busters would be sufficient, although it may require a second pass at a site such as Natanz. Apparently, the attack on Syria's nuclear operations in 2007 was an excellent test run.

While IDF F15s and F16s are deemed more than capable to destroy or cripple some of Iran's facilities, the underground site at Fordow might actually require ground forces in order to render it unusable for an undetermined period.

According to the German, "Israel's Air Force is first class. Their pilots are conditioned from the history of Israel and the constant dangers faced by the Jewish state."[183]

Conversely, one of Iran's strengths is a sizeable and assorted variety of long-range artillery rockets and ballistic missiles—perhaps the most diverse in the entire Middle East. In its war chest are an estimated 200-300 *Shahab*-1 and *Shahab*-2, widely known as SCUDs. Added to those are a significant number of *Zelzal* rockets and semi-guided rockets, the Fateh-110. While there may seem to be strength in numbers, the rockets in Iran's possession are not terribly accurate and would likely not be a decisive factor in a confrontation either with Israel or the United States. It would require several precise adjustments to improve the accuracy of Iran's missile stockpile. These are the missiles on which that country would have to rely if it were to target Israel.[184] There has been speculation that the proposed development of the *Sajjil-2* missile would give Iran an edge, but advancement on that project seems to have stalled—with only one known test flight of the *Sajjil-2* since 2009. Meanwhile, Iran's leaders, who apparently believe themselves indestructible, could cause a psychological stir if they were to lob the country's unnumbered store of rockets heavenward and just let them fall where they may. It is comparable to Charles Swindoll's description of Goliath, the giant of Gath:

Goliath reminds me of the cross-eyed discus thrower. He didn't set any records… but he sure kept the crowd awake![185]

The rockets could easily reach targets such as the coastal cities of Saudi Arabia and the cosmopolitan and wealthy city of Dubai. These are well within the range of the *Zelzal* rockets. It is possible that air defense installations provided by the U.S. for its allies in the GCC (Gulf Cooperation Council) could provide adequate protection, and at the end of any conflict, Iran would be left quite vulnerable. The council is comprised of Kuwait, the United Arab Emirates, Qatar, Bahrain, Oman and Saudi Arabia.

Truthfully, Iran is spouting threats and warnings backed by an aging air force fleet of pre-1979 fighter jets purchased during the reign of the Shah. It does include a few more-recent purchases of Russian MIGs and SU-24 jets, but all lack the modernization that would allow Iran to compete on level ground with the U.S. and its allies in the Middle East.

Another area lacking is in the country's early-warning and communications systems:

> Iranian pilots are short of Bottom of Form sophisticated airborne command-and-warning assets, as well as the secure communications network needed to relay vital threat and targeting information. These deficiencies place Iranian pilots at a grave disadvantage if engaged by better-equipped forces furnished with up-to-date maps.
>
> But likely the most major inadequacy lies in the trained manpower necessary to keep the fleet airborne. According to Realclearworld.com, Iran would be hindered by the ability to "generate anything beyond one sortie per day for each fighter jet."[186]

COUNTDOWN

 **4 SANCTIONS AND SHORTAGES**

CHAPTER SEVENTEEN
THE RIAL STOPS HERE

The Shah of Iran fell in 1979 followed in quick succession by the capture of the U.S. Embassy by rioters in Tehran. Fifty-two employees were taken hostage and held for 444 days. The U.S. began to lead global efforts to levy sanctions against the newly-formed theocratic republic, and its leader, the Ayatollah Ruhollah Khomeini. In the years following, the sanctions hampered the republic, but the bite wasn't deeply felt until 2011. That was when restrictive new sanctions were announced following Iran's refusal to allow inspections of its nuclear sites.

Unemployment in Iran has skyrocketed under the constraints:

> Iran's official unemployment rate is about 13 percent. But economists estimate the real figure is more than 20 percent.... Economists say Iran will have to create more than a million new jobs every year in order to accommodate its young population. But only about 300,000 new jobs are created each year, leaving the country's youth frustrated and disillusioned.[187]

In 2013, poverty plagued at least one of every four inhabitants, inflation was rampant and expected to increase even more based on President Ahmadinejad's determination to spend more with less money. An article in Foreign Affairs determined:

> If Washington wants to derail Iran's nuclear program, it

must take advantage of a split in Tehran between hard-liners, who care mostly about security, and pragmatists, who want to fix Iran's ailing economy. By promising strong rewards for compliance and severe penalties for defiance, Washington can strengthen the pragmatists' case that Tehran should choose butter over bombs.[188]

As of 2012, approximately 4.1 percent of U.S. citizens were on welfare. In Iran that figure is estimated to be as high at ninety percent, and that includes the particularly poverty-stricken villages and towns outside Tehran. Speculation is that because it is a young country in terms of median age, as many as a million young, educated men and women will be searching for employment. Private enterprise in Iran is all but non-existent—unless one is a cook, a farmer, or a waiter.

Having run for a second term on the promise to divide revenues from Iran's oil industry with the poorest in the country, Ahmadinejad, who because of term limits was forced to leave office after the June 2013 election, never made good on that statement. Those were not his only dishonored vows; he proposed to offer more loans to small businesses and to newlywed couples—that too has not happened at this writing. There is, of course, the possibility that after laying out for one four-year term, Ahmadinejad could be re-elected to office; that is permissible under Iranian law. According to the *Economist,* the opposite is true:

> The biggest looming issue is Mr. Ahmadinejad's plan to slash consumer subsidies that cost his government $70 billion-100 billion a year, a quarter of GDP. Already lumbered with feeble economic growth and high unemployment, Iranians now face the prospect of sharp rises in prices of food, fuel and transport.[189]

The countries worldwide that joined forces to impose sanctions on Iran did so in hopes of restricting the amount of currency available to purchase the materials and expertise needed to continue its nuclear pursuits. The opposite was true; nothing seemed, on the surface at least, to interfere with Khamenei and Ahmadinejad's determination to possess atomic weapons.

The weaker rial triggered a run on gold and foreign currency and further exacerbated the problem as Iranians withdrew savings in order to make their purchases. Iran's economy was further destabilized. People such as students, medical patients, and business owners seeking to purchase dollars or other foreign currencies were forced to prove need before a supply would be made available.

As closely tied to its oil market in terms of economics as is Iran, diversity should be the number one pursuit. The reliance on income from oil has made other Iranian exports less competitive globally, and broadens the damage to the nation's economy.

Iran's nuclear intransigence has resulted in a steady rise in crude prices globally. The economy has been in turmoil, an issue that doesn't escape its leaders. And with the worsening of conditions for the people of Iran, what are their greatest concerns? According to Karim Sadjadpour, an expert on Iran at the International Crisis Group:

> While some people may feel nationalistic, I can count just as many people who are concerned about this [nuclear] project or are ambivalent. And frankly, this is a very technical project—you know, the act of enriching uranium indigenously as opposed to importing enriched uranium from abroad. So the idea that your average Iranian waking up in the morning in Yazd or Shiraz says, you know, what's missing from my life is enriched uranium. [190]

In early 2012, President Ahmadinejad was forced to agree to increase Iran's interest rate to 21 percent causing the populace of his country to become increasingly worried about the economy and the toll on future income. It appeared that the sanctions imposed by world leaders were having the desired effect—although it is a concept foreign to Ahmadinejad.

According to various sources, the impact of the sanctions was supposed to bring Iran's oil industry to its knees. Not so! Countries such as Sri Lanka, China, Japan, Italy, South Korea, Spain, Greece, Turkey, and South Africa remained aloof and refused to join the United States and European Union in banning the import of Iranian crude. These countries represent a petroleum import ratio of anywhere from 10 percent to 100 percent. These nations are not willing to curtail imports just to please Western powers.

The pinch, however, is still being felt in the area of foreign currency sales. According to the IRNA news agency in Tehran, Iranians have been instructed to buy dollars only when traveling.

Hoarding of U.S. currency had become *de rigueur* in aristocratic circles in the country. It was the currency to covet, but no longer. Now it will be at a premium, and government permission will be required to purchase dollars. Ahmadinejad has acknowledged—albeit subtly—that the sanctions have seriously worsened the value of the Iranian rial. One anonymous Iranian politician depicted the current economy as the worst since the Iran/Iraq war.

Finance Minister Shamseddin Hosseini has indicated that sanctions imposed by the West had driven inflation over the 30 percent mark, although analysts indicate it could be even higher. He reiterated, however, that Iran would not halt its nuclear pursuits under any circumstances. I was reminded of a comment by the late Ayatollah Khomeini:

> "I say let this land [Iran] burn. I say let this land go up in smoke,
>   provided Islam emerges triumphant in the rest of the world."

Hosseini specified that the continuing sanctions on Iran's oil industry and central bank had produced a "currency shock" and that the rial had lost approximately 80 percent in value over a two-year time period. He reported that food prices had risen exponentially and cattle-raisers were being encouraged to butcher more stock.

The countries that joined forces to impose sanctions on Iran did so in hopes of restricting the amount of currency available to purchase the materials and expertise needed to continue its nuclear pursuits. The weaker rial triggered a run on gold and foreign currency and further exacerbated the problem as Iranians withdrew savings in order to make their purchases. Iran's economy has been further destabilized. People such as students, medical patients, and business owners seeking to purchase dollars or other foreign currencies would be forced to prove need before a supply could be made available. Raising the interest rate was a risky move on Ahmadinejad's part as inflation continues to rise despite the increase. It could have put his leadership position at risk in a parliament already critical of the despotic president—but once again Iran's own version of the "Teflon president" slid out of the grasp of his detractors.

The sanctions, far from causing the Iranians to rethink their resolute rush to gain nuclear weapons, resulted only in a more defiant attitude, and were labeled "ineffective." That would, of course, be more effective were China and India to join the list of countries imposing restrictions on Iran.

If the Iranian people grow tired of the government's machinations, could we see a repeat of the tactics used to overthrow the Shah of Iran? A weapon used by the Ayatollah Ruhollah Khomeini when he engineered the overthrow of the Shah was oil-related strikes. He took full advantage of the freedom to use the media for his purposes. The Ayatollah began to urge the workers in Iran— from oil workers to garbage haulers—to go on strike. Students were encouraged to riot in support of the working class. The strikes proved to be very efficient at creating dissention. The strikes spread from the Tehran oil refinery to the oil refineries at Isfahan, Abadan, Tabriz, and Sharaz. In one week, oil production fell by three million barrels.

Should the Iranian people again employ that strategy against their government, blood will flow in the streets of the villages, towns, and cities of that country. When the people revolted following Ahmadinejad's re-election in 2009, the U.S. government and the Obama administration did nothing to help them defend themselves against reprisals. They would likely be very reluctant to try a second time unless the U.S. were to rally behind them and the Western press was supportive. Without that, there is little chance of revolution in Iran.

Will sanctions eventually be a strong deterrent? It has long been thought by politicos that they are not effective. That idea can be supported by gauging their effectiveness against Fidel Castro who quickly established a dictatorship on the island nation of Cuba despite sanctions imposed. However, in recent years, the perception that sanctions don't work has been disproven by their effectiveness against North Korea.

Why have these newest attempts been more effective? The USA Patriot

Act, Section 311, allows the United States Treasury to label foreign banks as being of "primary money laundering concern."[191] This prevents the institution from being a clearing house for U.S. dollars; disallowing any transactions with banks, and for that matter, halting any affiliation with American financial institutions. This proverbial shot-in-the-arm in applying monetary sanctions effectively quarantines the targeted country and keeps it from infecting other banks worldwide. This is due in large part to globalization, another tool which could be effective in isolating Iran.

In September 2006, the U.S. Treasury department targeted one of Iran's largest government banks—Bank Saderat. The bank was charged with channeling approximately $50 million in payments to terrorist organizations Hezbollah and Hamas. All contact with the U.S. banking system was shut off. Similar actions were taken in January 2007 against Bank Sepah in order to slow Iran's purchases of ballistic missiles.

Washington Post reporter David Ignatius summed up these moves by the U.S. Treasury:

> The new sanctions are toxic because they effectively limit a country's access to the global ATM. In that sense, they impose— at last—a real price on countries such as North Korea and Iran that have blithely defied UN resolutions on proliferation. "What's the goal?" asks [Treasury spokesperson, Stuart] Levey. "To create an internal debate about whether these policies [of defiance] make sense. And that's happening in Iran. People with business sense realize that this conduct makes it hard to continue normal business relationships."[192]

Although sanctions imposed by the UN have generated little response, that organization has gathered some support from China and Russia, as well as the EU and U.S, which have all released statements supporting the determination that Iran should be banned from possessing nuclear weapons. As well, U.S. financial sanctions, "creatively administered by the Treasury Department, are working to discourage European and Japanese banks from financing important projects in Iran, and are having an adverse impact on Iran's economy."[193]

CHAPTER EIGHTEEN

BLACK GOLD—OILING THE WHEELS OF TERROR

According to one European shipping industry source, oil is so plentiful in Iran that it is now being stored in tankers along the shores of the Persian Gulf. Reuter's reported in April 2013:

> "There is no doubt there are more Iranian tankers being used for floating storage at the moment on their side of the Gulf and the feeling is this is expected to rise....The embargo is hurting and there has been talk of attempts by Iran to unload oil cargoes at distressed prices."[194]

No one knows with absolute certainty just how much of Iran's oil supply is lying offshore in as many as ten of the country's flotilla, but the estimate is that quantities are high. According to an April 2013 article in the *Jerusalem Post*:

> The vessels, all belonging to Iran's top tanker operator NITC, were located close to the Iranian oil terminals of Assaluyeh, Kharg Island and Bahregan, the data showed. "There seem to be more vessels than there were four

months ago - the big area which seems to have changed is
off Assaluyeh," said Richard Hurley, a senior analyst at IHS
Fairplay....There are more ships that seem to have come in
to that anchorage in the past four months or so. At one point
they were down to a core storage fleet of around six vessels
anchored off Kharg Island and Assaluyeh."

It seems apparent to the trained eye that sanctions are not only hurting
Iran's general economy, but are prompting the downfall of its oil production
and exports. The government has resorted to raising prices to counteract
losses, but the countries that rely strongly on imports from Iran are bearing
the brunt of the rising costs.

According to the U.S. Energy Department:

In 2012, Iran's exports of crude oil and lease condensate
dropped to their lowest level since 1986 as the United States
and the European Union (EU) tightened sanctions targeting
Iran's oil sector. Iran's 2012 net estimated oil export revenue,
at $69 billion, was significantly lower than the $95 billion
total generated in 2011. Oil exports make up 80% of Iran's
total export earnings and 50% to 60% of its government revenue, according to the Economist Intelligence Unit.[195]

The lack of revenue could seriously hamper Iran's continued ability
to purchase arms and equipment not only for its own country, but for its
proxies that depend on the influx of income to sustain terrorist activities. It
could also become increasingly more difficult to recover from an attack on
its nuclear sites by Israel.

Added to the drop in oil income were new sanctions enacted in April
2013, and an avowal by European underwriters to stop covering Iranian
refineries. According to the U.S. Department of Energy:

"The new provision will mostly affect refiners in South
Korea and India, which rely heavily on European insurance

providers. The new sanctions may further affect Iran's exports and production over the next few months as refiners try to find alternative suppliers of insurance."[196]

By the end of 2013, the Iranian government could very well be awash in crude as demands in Asia weaken. This is particularly indicative of the signs of the times especially as China has surpassed the United States in the total number of barrels imported. This is due, in part, to the resurgence of oil exploration and reclamation on the U.S. mainland. Experts and analysts from the intelligence community see this as a positive step for a country heavily dependent on foreign oil imports. Dan Yergin, energy analyst and author, saw the change in attitude at the World Economic Forum in Switzerland in January 2013:

> "People already are looking at the U.S. differently, seeing the U.S. as much more competitive in the world."[197]

Gleaning a great harvest from new technological advances in unlocking latent oil and gas reserves in the continental United States, a dream born in 1973, could be realized in another decade: Total energy independence. When combined with increasing demands that carmakers manufacture more energy efficient vehicles and the introduction of more green products, odds favor a further reduction in crude imports.

Although Iranian exports to an oil-hungry globe have dropped more than 1.5 million barrels per day, "North Dakota, Ohio, and Pennsylvania together produced 1.5 million barrels of oil a day."[198]

Dan Yergin reiterated the importance of that achievement:

> People talk of the future impact. The increase in U.S oil production has already had an impact: Sanctions wouldn't have been effective without U.S. oil production. ... We've added (within the last year) almost as much as Iran was exporting before sanctions."[199]

If the U.S. continues to achieve its stated goal of energy autonomy, the stranglehold of the OPEC nations could be broken with its members the biggest losers. Daniel Gallington, Senior Policy and Program Adviser at the George C. Marshall Institute in Arlington, Virginia, believes:

> A dramatic expansion of U.S. production could also push global spare capacity to exceed 8 million barrels per day, at which point OPEC could lose price control and crude oil prices would drop, possibly sharply. Such a drop would take a heavy toll on many energy producers who are increasingly dependent on relatively high energy prices to balance their budgets.[200]

Another issue to be addressed when contemplating the question of how the West can be saved from an apocalyptic event orchestrated by Iran is that of globalization. What is it and what effect might it have on saving the West from Iran's nuclear pursuits and apocalyptic mission? Globalization is defined as:

> A process of interaction and integration among the people, companies, and governments of different nations, a process driven by international trade and investment and aided by information technology. This process has effects on the environment, on culture, on political systems, on economic development and prosperity, and on human physical well-being in societies around the world.[201]

Globalization knows no borders and crosses international boundaries. That is why the fight against terrorism in any form must first be global. No one is exempt from the hatred and fanaticism that grips radical Islamic countries such as Iran. Having explored the dangers of nuclear weapons in the hands of leaders such as those in power in Tehran, we must define ways in which the world community can halt the forward progress of an atomic Iran.

A unified world marketplace would have a major impact on the economy of Iran. Such global tools as the Internet, Twitter, Facebook, and others are used by terrorist groups to plot and plan strikes, to fundraise, and to engage new members; those same tools could be used to discourage trade with Iran. Globalization could be a vital tool in halting the forward march toward an apocalypse, but only if world leaders are engaged. It directly affects markets, economies, communications, transportation, trade, service industries, and capital. It clearly could be a determining factor in whether or not sanctions against Iran were effective. It could be used to leverage Iran's oil-based economy.

In a speech delivered at the National Defense College graduation ceremony in July 2009, Benjamin Netanyahu addressed the effectiveness of globalization:

> Eventually radical Islam will be defeated by the global information revolution, by the freedom of ideas which are breaking out, through technology and through ideas of freedom. This won't happen immediately, but it will happen... The only thing that can postpone and disrupt the rate of the extinguishing of radical Islam is the possibility that it will be armed with a nuclear weapon.[202]

While there are those who feel that "globalization" is a word not to be used in polite company or in political circles, it might well be a most effective weapon against Iran if wielded unilaterally. It would require a united front which would of necessity include China and Russia, not to mention a decline in the purchase of crude from the Iranian oil wells, and could, as suggested be a possible key to halting an atomic Iran. If Iran continues on the course of nuclear proliferation the U.S. government must quickly take the extreme measure of a complete oil embargo, not allowing fuel to be sold by Iran or refined petroleum to be delivered to the country. This would further collapse the economy of the Islamic terror state.

These are all things that could work against Iran: Sanctions, engaging Russia and China, globalization techniques, and a refined oil embargo. These are all tools that could be instrumental in intercepting the countdown to Armageddon and saving the West from an Iranian-induced apocalypse.

COUNTDOWN

3 THE PROXY WARS

CHAPTER NINETEEN

WAR BY PROXY—FAMILIARITY BREEDS ATTEMPT

While some may categorize the threat from Iran as minimal, it would certainly not be Yuval Steinitz, the man who served as Israeli Strategic Affairs Minister in 2013, and is very well aware of Iran's proxy wars. At a conference in New York City in April of that year, Steinitz declared that Iran, and its nuclear ambition, was the most pressing problem in the world today.

Steinitz was adamant that the threat of a regime such as that in Iran could not and should not be downplayed—that multitudes of people in Japan, South Korea, and Alaska would be "living under a tangible and serious nuclear threat."[203] He noted that Winston Churchill had tried to warn the European community of the danger inherent in allowing Germany to rearm after World War I—with disastrous results.

Steinitz was convinced that "if Iran gets the first few bombs, in a decade or so they will have 100 nuclear bombs," and therefore Iran will be equal to "30 nuclear North Koreas."[204] He, like many, is concerned by the possibility that Iran's ambition to form a new global caliphate will bring to bear a new wave Islamic domination. Regarding increased sanctions, he added:

> "What is now necessary is to paint a very clear military
> threat, a credible threat that will make it crystal clear that

they are paying something for nothing. Only the combination of strong sanctions on the one hand and a red-line[d]
military threat on the other hand will create an impossible
situation" for Tehran. "If there is a chance to resolve this
problem without military action," he said, it will only be
because opponents of Tehran's nuclear program "choose a
big enough stick and wave it in their faces."[205]

To use the words of Turkish Prime Minister Recep Erdogan, Israel took
"precaution to act in a timely and quick manner against additional risks and
threats" to its populace. Its brief incursion into Syrian airspace was intended
to block the shipment of dangerous arms out of Syria to the Hezbollah jihadists, who had menacingly warned Israelis that Hezbollah's rockets had the
capability of costing them "tens of thousands of dead."

In late January 2013, Israel struck inside the confines of Syria. The
target was a convoy thought to be transporting anti-aircraft weapons from
Iran to Hezbollah in Lebanon. The air strike was aimed at a site close to
Lebanon's border. The contents of the caravan were also believed to be highly
sophisticated rockets capable of carrying chemical weapons intended for use
against Israel— matériel that could impede Israel's self-defense capabilities.
The strike did not go unnoticed by the Iranians. According to information
from the Middle East Media Research Institute (MEMRI):

> On February 13, 2013, Mehdi Taeb, the head of Iranian
> Supreme Leader Ali Khamenei's Ammar Base think tank and
> the brother of Islamic Revolutionary Guard Corps (IRGC)
> intelligence bureau director Hossein Taeb, delivered a speech
> at a Basij conference in Mashhad, Iran, on Syria's importance
> to the Iranian regime. In his speech, he defined Syria as a
> strategic Iranian province, and said that preserving the exis-
> tence of the Syrian regime was even more important to the
> Iranian regime than preserving the oil-rich southern Iranian
> province of Khuzestan–despite the latter's strategic and eco-
> nomic importance. Taeb also stressed that if Iran's enemies

were to attack both Syria and Khuzestan, Tehran would pre-
fer to preserve Syria, since its loss would lead to the loss of
Tehran itself. He added that Iran had helped to establish a
60,000-man Basij force in Syria which is fighting the rebels
alongside the regime of Syrian President Bashar Al-Assad.[206]

Israel halted fighting against Hezbollah in 2006 with assurances that
the free flow of arms to its sworn enemy would be stopped. When the exact
opposite was observed year after year, Israel determined that it could no
longer stand silently by and allow its citizens to be bombarded with threats
of death and destruction.

In December 2012, Ron Proser, UN Ambassador from Israel, called on
the Security Council to not ignore Hezbollah's weapons stockpile, a distinct
breach of an embargo that had been in place since 2006. Said the ambassador:

> In flagrant breach of (Security Council) resolution 1701,
> Hezbollah has built its arsenal to unprecedented levels,
> amassing 50,000 deadly missiles in Lebanon—more mis-
> siles than many NATO members have in their possession.
> These missiles can reach all of Israel and well beyond....I
> call on the Security Council and all responsible members
> of the international community to send a clear signal that
> Hezbollah's rapid rearmament will not be tolerated—backed
> by concrete steps on the ground. A logical first step is to
> ensure that Hezbollah is placed on relevant terrorism watch
> lists in all corners of the globe, including in the European
> Union."[207]

As it became more apparent that the UN Security Council had failed to
enforce its own edicts, Israel determined it had to step in to insure its own
protection in January 2013, and again in May of the same year when Israel
was again forced to target additional arms destined for Hezbollah. Following
the second strike, Aaron Sagui, Israeli Embassy spokesperson said only that
"Israel is determined to prevent the transfer of chemical weapons or other

game-changing weaponry by the Syrian regime to terrorists, especially to Hezbollah in Lebanon."[208]

Policies of the Iranian government which allow the export of its fanatical ideologies to other rogue countries globally will not halt unless or until nations worldwide adopt the fitting and proper mindset toward terrorism. Funding and employment of proxies such as Hezbollah, Hamas, and other overzealous organizations serve a purpose in Iran's arsenal of unconventional weapons used against Israel and the West.

Each faction has its own little mission, unique to the location and situation, but all in the name of its host, Iran. Hamas brazenly attacks Israel without warning or provocation; Hezbollah provides arms and training for the thousands dedicated to destruction, and other, smaller groups have, like bloodthirsty leeches, attached to the body in order to suck it dry of support. One such organization is the Palestinian Islamic Jihad in Syria—a Hamas wannabe dedicated to annihilating Israel by any means possible. Each of the deadly vipers that slither around in the name of Iran's Qods force is busily grasping every ounce of training and funding available.

The Shi'ite faction, Hezbollah, came to prominence in 1982 with an ideology based on that of Ayatollah Ruhollah Khomeini. It has, over the years, become an invaluable instrument in the hands of Iran's puppet masters. Employing plausible deniability, Iran's Supreme Leader, Ali Khamenei, can manipulate and maneuver Hezbollah to do his bidding in covert military operations while presenting an innocent, "Who, me?" face to the world at large.[209]

Even as Hezbollah has withdrawn to a degree from using terrorism as its primary source of disruption, the convoluted trail of funding and arms supplies eventually leads to Iran. The group's leader, Hassan Nasrallah, could be called upon at any time to reignite the Israel/Lebanon war and begin to employ the thousands and thousands of rockets Iran has smuggled into arms depots in southern Lebanon. Hezbollah is an arrow in Iran's arsenal of weapons, and its leaders will not hesitate to call in the markers when needed against Israel. According to Nasrallah:

> "We in the resistance inform that we are ready to receive
> quality weapon... with which we will fight the aggression

against our people, our land and our holy sites. We stand
together with the Syrian resistance and will offer assistance
and training in order to free the occupied Syrian Golan."[210]

He has vowed that Hezbollah would "move to order rocket fire in retaliation for every Israeli strike."[211]

Hamas, on the other hand, makes no pretense of being moderate; it has one aim—the total annihilation of the Jewish state—and no hesitation in employing any means available to achieve that goal. That was never more obvious than in 2011 when Hamas terrorists attacked a school bus delivering children to their homes at the end of the school day.

The gleaming yellow bus had made its last stop near the Kibbutz Sa'ad when a Russian-made *Kornet*, a laser-guided weapon was launched from Gaza. Only one sixteen-year old young man, Daniel Wipliech, remained on the bus with the driver, Zion Yemini, when the rocket hit the back of the vehicle. As shrapnel exploded through the confines of the bus, it tore through Daniel causing massive wounds to his head, neck, and body, and triggering massive blood loss.

As the paramedics arrived on the scene, Hamas launched a secondary attack on the first responders. While pinned down in the wreckage, Daniel stopped breathing, but was resuscitated and eventually transported to a medical center. Ten days later, the young man died.[212] Initially, Hamas denied targeting the school bus, but later claimed responsibility—as the world looked on in silence at the death of another innocent Israeli child. This is the group that is backed solidly by the Iranian government.

Few doubt that Iran's leaders will persist in supporting groups such as Hamas and Hezbollah, and nations such as Syria and North Korea to further their agenda of world domination. How long will the strategy continue? It will spread its venomous influence as long as the Western allies continue to sit on the fence and refuse to take action against the bully that is Iran. Until and unless someone in the international arena develops a backbone steely enough to say, "Enough!" the charade will continue and the world will move ever more closely to a nuclear Armageddon—Iran-style.

Lest the world think Iran will turn its back on Syria, Israel's neighbor on the north, the two countries have a mutual defense treaty complete with a pledge to defend Damascus if needed. Ayatollah Khamenei and his crowd have a vested interested in keeping Syria in its quiver; its loss would mean the Shi'ite stronghold would no longer have a pathway to the Mediterranean Sea—a strategy in keeping with the desire to dominate the region.

If the unvarnished truth were acknowledged, Arab entities in the Middle East would be delighted were Israel to stop the bully in its tracks. Fearful that sanctions were not really effective, Saudi Foreign Minister Prince Saud al-Faisal revealed to then-Secretary of State Hillary Clinton that bombing Iran was preferable to Iran having nuclear weapons. That admission sent shockwaves across the Middle East and uncovered the dirty little secret—Israel was welcome to tackle Iran. The minister backpedaled, of course, when confronted, but not before the genii was out of the bottle. The reality is that if the United States doesn't step up to the plate, Israel may have a new Goliath to face.

COUNTDOWN

2 SPIRIT WARS

CHAPTER TWENTY

BUT THE PRINCE OF THE KINGDOM OF PERSIA WITHSTOOD ME...[213]

A 2013 report from both the *Wall Street Journal* and *Haaretz* announced that the United States had developed a "bunker buster penetrator bomb"[214] that would decimate Iran's nuclear enrichment site at Fordow. It had been thought to be too well-fortified to even consider an assault. The bomb which would deplete federal coffers by hundreds of millions of dollars would be germane in any plan to bomb Iran's atomic program. Apparently concerned that Israel could not effectively deliver a knock-out blow with its current conventional weapons, the Pentagon set to work redesigning the bomb in order to attack Iranian below-surface installations.

Secretary of Defense Chuck Hagel reportedly reassured the Israeli government that while trying to reach a solution through sanctions, military responses were not off the table. He intimated that the Obama administration would continue with diplomatic efforts through the Iranian elections scheduled for June 14, 2013, but would reassess options after that time.

In actuality, almost every military expert feels that within a decade of Iran developing the atomic bomb, we will have a nuclear "Armageddon" in the Middle East. That timeline is eerily close to Dr. Tim LaHaye's belief that we will only have a little more than a decade between the attack of Gog's coalition and Jesus Christ's return. I don't think any of the experts realize that this is no exaggeration. Once Iran has nuclear weapons, I can't see anything else stopping it from attacking Israel exactly as foretold in Ezekiel 38-39.

Ezekiel describes what God shows him will happen:

> "In My zeal and in My blazing wrath I declare that on that day there will surely be a great earthquake in the land of Israel. The fish of the sea, the birds of the heavens, the beasts of the field, all the creeping things that creep on the earth, and all the men who are on the face of the earth will shake at My presence; the mountains also will be thrown down, the steep pathways will collapse and every wall will fall to the ground. I will call for a sword against him on all My mountains," declares the Lord God. "Every man's sword will be against his brother. With pestilence and with blood I will enter into judgment with him; and I will rain on him and on his troops, and on the many peoples who are with him, a torrential rain, with hailstones, fire and brimstone.
>
> "I will strike your bow from your left hand and dash down your arrows from your right hand [referring to aircraft, launchers, rockets, and missiles?]. You will fall on the mountains of Israel, you and all your troops and the peoples who are with you; I will give you as food to every kind of predatory bird and beast of the field.
>
> "On that day I will give Gog a burial ground there in Israel, the valley of those who pass by east of the sea, and it will block off those who would pass by. So they will bury Gog there with all his horde, and they will call it the valley of Hamon-gog. For seven months the house of Israel will be burying them in order to cleanse the land. Even all the people of the land will bury them; and it will be to their renown on the day that I glorify Myself," declares the Lord God. (Ezekiel 38:19-22; 39:3-4, 11-13)

The defeat of Gog's army at the very moment of victory will be so miraculous, providentially timed, and sudden, that the world will recognize it was the power of God that delivered Israel. Joel 2:20 seems to describe this defeat as well:

> "But I will remove the northern army far from you,
> And I will drive it into a parched and desolate land,
> And its vanguard into the eastern sea,
> And its rear guard into the western sea.
> And its stench will arise and its foul smell will come up,
> For it has done great things."

Certainly there will be detractors and skeptics who defend the defeat of the Russo-Iranian coalition as a series of unfortunate events, but that argument will only hold water with the most defiant opponents of God's existence. Tremors of revival—which, as we have discussed, are already being felt today—will sweep the Earth and grow until all true believers in Jesus Christ are caught up in the Rapture.

As this revival is taking place, Israel will have years of cleanup work to do. Some translations make reference to "The Valley of the Travelers" in reference to where Hamon-gog will be. For example, in the *English Standard Version*, Ezekiel 39:11 reads:

> "On that day I will give to Gog a place for burial in Israel,
> the Valley of the Travelers, east of the sea. It will block the
> travelers, for there Gog and all his multitude will be buried.
> It will be called the Valley of Hamon-gog."

It is believed that the Valley of the Travelers refers to the ancient trade route that spanned from Aqaba at the tip of the Red Sea in the south, through Petra and Amman east of the Dead Sea, the Jordan River, and the Sea of Galilee, all the way to Damascus. It was part of what was called "The King's Highway" or "The Desert Highway," and was referred to in Numbers 20. According to *The Treasury of Scriptural Knowledge*, the Valley of Hamon-Gog is:

Probably the valley near the Sea of Gennesareth [Galilee], as the Targum renders, and so-called because it was the great road by which the merchants and traders from Syria and other Eastern countries went into Egypt. Perhaps what is now called the plains of Haouran, south of Damascus.[215]

The Plains of Haouran is a great expanse that includes the Valley of Tears; it is located east of the Golan Heights and the Sea of Galilee. Most of the debris from Gog's aircraft and missiles will fall on troops gathered in this valley, while others will fall on the mountains of Jerusalem as far as they could penetrate before God intervenes.

After Gog's defeat, this valley will be impassible, possibly choked with toxins from chemical and biological weapons that will likely impact Damascus. (It is less than fifty miles from the Israeli border near the Golan Heights to Damascus.) The implication here is that after the battle, the devastated battlefield will become annexed by Israel as a burial ground. For seven months, workers in hazmat suits will walk this plain, gathering and burying the dead. The number buried there will be so many that the nearest village will be renamed "*Hamonah*" (Ezekiel 39:16)—which means "multitudes"—that will serve as a place of hotels and restaurants to care for those coming to visit the memorial cemetery. In the months beyond that:

> "Then those who inhabit the cities of Israel will go out and make fires with the weapons and burn them, both shields and bucklers, bows and arrows, war clubs and spears, and for seven years they will make fires of them. They will not take wood from the field or gather firewood from the forests, for they will make fires with the weapons; and they will take the spoil of those who despoiled them and seize the plunder of those who plundered them," declares the Lord God. (Ezekiel 39:9-10)

The nations that had sought to plunder Israel will instead have left weapons, fuel, scrap metal, and other resources to be salvaged by the Israelis. It seems more likely they will salvage figurative rather than actual wood, but it is hard to say. As the salvagers clear out the wreckage, they will set up markers as they find new bodies, so that those can be collected and buried as well. (See Ezekiel 39:15.)

It is this part of the prophecy—that resources left by Gog's decimated army will be gathered for seven years—that made Tim LaHaye believe the latest this battle could be waged would be three and a half years before the beginning of the Tribulation, or seven years before the Abomination of Desolation and the beginning of the Great Tribulation, a time in which the Jewish population will be fleeing for their lives and will go into hiding. In other words, the seven-year burial and gathering period will overlap the first half of the Tribulation.

It also seems likely there would be a period of years before the Rapture— which I believe will happen just prior to the beginning of Daniel's Seventieth Week (and the beginning of the Tribulation)—allowing that "This gospel of the kingdom shall be preached in the whole world as a testimony to all the nations, and then the end will come" (Matthew 24:14). Israel will experience a time of relative peace again, in which God will work in their midst, returning His people to Himself, along with many others around the world.

"And I will set My glory among the nations; and all the nations will see My judgment which I have executed and My hand which I have laid on them. And the house of Israel will know that I am the Lord their God from that day onward. The nations will know that the house of Israel went into exile for their iniquity because they acted treacherously against Me, and I hid My face from them; so I gave them into the hand of their adversaries, and all of them fell by the sword. According to their uncleanness and according to their transgressions I dealt with them, and I hid My face from them."

Therefore thus says the Lord God, "Now I will restore the fortunes of Jacob and have mercy on the whole house of Israel; and I will be jealous for My holy name. They will forget their disgrace and all their treachery which they perpetrated against Me, when they live securely on their own land with no one to make them afraid. When I bring them back from the peoples and gather them from the lands of their enemies, then I shall be sanctified through them in the sight of the many nations. Then they will know that I am the Lord their God because I made them go into exile among the nations, and then gathered them again to their own land; and I will leave none of them there any longer. I will not hide My face from them any longer, for I will have poured out My Spirit on the house of Israel," declares the Lord God. (Ezekiel 39:21-29)

In the aftermath of this war, the influence of nations of Gog's coalition will be all but extinguished. In a world that is suddenly without Russia and the main financier of radical Shi'a Islam, Iran, the power blocks will become the West, China, and the Sunni nations of the Arabian Peninsula with the rejuvenated Iraq at its forefront. Al Qaeda has already fallen with the death of Bin Laden and will not likely rise again to its former prominence.

The world—likely through a body such as the U.N.—will take a renewed interested in maintaining the peace of the Middle East because it was the host of this battle, and the most likely seat open for outside forces to make a home will be in Iraq. The rebuilding of Babylon could easily be the compromise to allow for this. As a sign to the world of their dedication to this aim, a united "world caliphate" will indeed rise out of the ashes of ancient Babylon, only it will not be a Shi'a messiah who initiates this unification. Instead it will be someone out of the last ruler seen in Daniel's vision of the statue. From the "clay and iron" remnants of the Roman Empire—the European Union—will arise a world leader who will seek to make the world one. He will unify all nations under one flag and all religions under the one all-encompassing Universalist doctrine. Today we can already see the forerunner in such teachings as the New Age and twisted metaphysics dogma.

It seems likely we will be around for at least part of the move to this, with the ultimate rise of this Antichrist. The acceptance of this counterfeit leader will be further facilitated by the final disappearance at the Rapture of all dissenting voices. For what will be left when the Church goes? The world is likely to see a huge shift to the political left, and the ultimate outcome of that cannot be pretty. The defeat of Gog's coalition will be an even more vivid sign of the coming of the last days than was the rebirth of the state of Israel. I truly believe it is the next great prophetic event, and as such, we need to be ready to act on God's behalf now, because once that happens it will likely be too late to start.

Before I close this chapter, I want to say that I am not a military analyst or expert on what needs to be done to invade or defend a country. My "imaginings" about what the attack of Gog might look like are formed only by what I have read of history, in the newspapers, and what comes to mind as I meditate on the Scriptures. What Ezekiel saw and described as "arrows," "horses," "shield and buckler," "swords," and "war clubs and spears", your guess is as good as mine. Did God give him a vision of these things in a way that he could understand in his own time, or did he look at men with machine guns riding in armored personnel carriers and describe them as a mounted cavalry? It is impossible to say. However, I feel it is valid to search these scriptures and see exactly how they might be fulfilled by examining what we do know.

Seeing how easily these prophecies could come about as things stand today adds one more set of signs that help determine the times in which we live. It is hard to look at these reports of earthquakes, a watering down of the Gospel among churches, false messiahs, and a Russo-Iranian alliance that sees itself called by Allah to wipe Israel from the face of the map, and not feel an urgency to be doing God's will every day without exception.

As I see it, there is no more time to wonder if Jesus is coming back soon. As these signs accelerate, if we don't start living like each day is our last day on Earth, we will miss the chance to act. When we see the signs of Matthew 24, it stresses all the more that we should be living the life of Matthew 25. The knowledge that Jesus is coming soon should not have us hoarding canned goods and heading for caves in the mountains to wait out His coming. It is a time to follow Him like those in the book of Acts did—a time to keep in step with the Holy Spirit as He works on the Earth for the final harvest of the Church Age. It is time to be the Christians we have always wanted to be, answering God's call and obeying as He speaks. If we do this, we face a very exciting time ahead!

Once again, these are not all the signs. If only these things were happening, there might be room for doubt; but there are other factors that indicate dramatic change is on the horizon. End-time prophecy also speaks of a monumental financial collapse that also may contribute to why Russia and its coalition attack Israel, or it may create a period of world war and unrest that will usher in the need for a one-world government to restore the peace. This will then pave the way for the leader (the Antichrist) who will come to power to end war and make a peace treaty with Israel that will last for seven years. On that day, the Tribulation will begin.

This economic chaos and the negotiated peace in Israel will be two other game changers that will mark the end of the Age. Will the actions of the Church be a third one? Certainly what God prophecies *will happen* whether we get involved or not, but we also have the potential to have an incredible impact in how these things affect individuals. Do we sit idly by and wait for Jesus to save us, or do we get involved through prayer and action just as Daniel did in his time? Do we choose to let the earth be "decimated" because so many are taken in the Rapture, or do we leave our neighbors to the wrath poured out in the Tribulation?

It is my conviction that we must act, and we must do what we can to help people weather the next two great crises: economic chaos and the outcome of negotiations between the Palestinians and Israelis. How likely are we to face such things? Where are we to stand? What forms are they likely to take? Are there already precursors happening in today's events? We will explore those questions in the next section.

COUNTDOWN

1 SIGNS OF THINGS TO COME

CHAPTER TWENTY-ONE
ARMAGEDDON BEGINS

Yossi Kollek stepped from the shower and toweled off. Through the bathroom window he could see the sun just peeking over the hills to the east and his mind turned to the training mission he would fly that day. As a pilot in the Israeli Air Force, he'd long since come to love morning flights. Never one for sleeping late or lounging around, he enjoyed the cool freshness of the new day and the sense of awakening that came with each sunrise. Plus, morning flights left afternoons free to do as he pleased. Now with a family, and with children approaching their teenage years, he valued the extra time at home.

Kollek glanced at the wristwatch that lay on the shelf above the sink. It was a little before six. If they followed the training schedule, they would be airborne by seven.

Twenty minutes later, he arrived at the main gate to Ramon Air Base. A guard checked his identification card, while someone searched beneath the vehicle and dogs sniffed for explosives. Then they waved him past the gate and he drove from the checkpoint. Minutes later, he turned into the parking lot outside a nondescript hangar that sat alongside one of the runways. He grabbed his flight bag from the front seat of the car and made his way inside the building to the ready room.

As he entered the room, he expected to see the usual dry eraser boards with information and directions about the morning's training exercise. Instead, he found the base commander standing at the head of the room. Rows of seats that lined the room were filled to capacity. Men unable to sit stood along the wall taking every space all the way around. Kollek squeezed into a spot near the door. "What's going on?" he asked the man next to him.

"I don't know," he shrugged. "Looks like they called everyone in who wasn't already on the schedule."

When everyone was assembled, the commander addressed the group. "Gentlemen, we have a slight change in plans today." He nodded to a man who stood to the left. "Sergeant Zurer will be coming around with bags for your cell phones. We need you to place them in one of the bags. Seal it. Print your name on the outside and then place the sealed bag in the basket that Major Geffen will be passing around."

"Major Geffen," someone called in jest. "Totin' the basket for Zurer." Geffen responded with a good-natured smile and a mock bow. Laughter rippled through the room.

"All right," the commander said in a flat, monotone. "Let's knock it off." He waited for the room to grow quiet, then continued. "From this point on, there will be no cell phones, no text messages, no email. Anyone caught with a cell phone, anyone caught making a call on a cell phone, anyone sending text messages or emails will be arrested, and I promise you it will be the end of your career."

The commander stepped aside and Colonel Tayeb spoke up. "Okay. There will be a change in the training schedule and we will meet back here at 0300 for the briefing. Until then, you will assemble with your flight group leaders. They will give you further instructions."

Murmuring began almost immediately as everyone realized they would have to remain on base. Kollek glanced across the room and saw Yoel Mintz leaning against the wall. He made his way to him. "What's this about?"

"Something really big."

"Another exercise?"

"I do not think so."

"Do you know?"

"No." Mintz shook his head.

"But you know something."

"No one knows anything yet."

"I'm supposed to attend my daughter's recital tonight. She'll be disappointed if I'm not there."

"No one gets off the base."

"I need to let them know I won't be home."

"The Comm Center is conveying that information right now."

Kollek was puzzled. "What are we doing?"

Mintz pushed away from the wall. "We're meeting down the hall in one of the classrooms. Get the others. I'll be down there waiting for you." He turned toward the door. "We have some details we must go over."

✧ ✧ ✧

(Ramon Air Base, Beersheba, Israel) Yossi Kollek sat in the cockpit of his F-16 and stared up at the sky. In the briefing room they said this wasn't a drill, but they didn't have to tell anyone. They all knew it as soon as cell phones were collected and everyone was confined to base. Now, they were on the taxiway and ready to go. The *Eitan* drone was more than an hour ahead of them. By now it was well inside Iraqi airspace, maybe even all the way to Iran. With it, radar and communications systems would be rendered useless. Only the Iranian air force could stop the attack now, and even it was no match for what was headed their way.

On the tarmac, telltale lights blinked on the wingtips of the planes that would accompany Yossi. Each aircraft in his group was armed with two of the most recent bunker-busting bombs. Designed to penetrate hardened underground facilities of any strength, they hung beneath the belly of the planes. On each of the wings, special racks held three five-hundred-pound bombs. More than enough firepower to destroy their assigned targets.

For an instant, Yossi's mind raced back to his family asleep in bed at home. He had missed his daughter's recital the evening before. He hoped they got the message that he was okay. In a few hours they would rise to meet the day. Breakfast, school, and his son's soccer game later in the afternoon. If he returned by … Yossi pushed the thought from his mind. "I must focus on the matter at hand," he told himself.

From the maps Mintz used in the flight group briefing, Yossi knew this was an all-out attack, a preemptive strike to destroy Iran's nuclear capability. Unlike the surgical bombing of the past, this time there would be no doubt about the origin of the attack. He wasn't told the extent of the mission but he was sure that dozens of other aircraft were leaving from bases all across the country. All those planes, hitting all those targets, would leave little room for ambiguity about who had actually sent them or the locations they struck.

Then the radio in Yossi's flight helmet crackled. "Strike leader. You are cleared for takeoff."

"Roger," Yossi replied. "Clear for takeoff." With his right hand he nudged the throttle forward and steered the plane onto the runway. Two F-16s took up positions with him, one at either end of his wingtips.

In the headset he heard the voice of a pilot, "This is it?"

"This is it," Yossi replied. Then he shoved the throttle forward and the jet engine burst to life. In a matter of seconds, the three planes shot down the runway and rose into the sky. Once aloft, they circled the air base twice as the sortie assembled. When all twenty-five planes were in place, they banked to the north and headed up the Mediterranean coast.

Moments later, a voice spoke in Yossi's headset. "What about the Syrians?"

"The Americans have them covered," someone replied.

"Cut the chatter, guys," Yossi cautioned.

At the border, they entered Syrian air space and adjusted their course to the east, on a path that took them directly over Aleppo. A few minutes later, the planes crossed into Iraqi airspace west of Tel Afar. So far, their flight had taken less than half an hour.

When they reached the border with Iran, Yossi keyed the microphone. "Departure point approaching."

One by one the group broke into teams. Yossi checked his course and confirmed the onboard computer's target information. His team was headed to a uranium processing plant at Isfahan. The others would hit the uranium enrichment plants at Natanz and Tabas, the heavy water facility at Arak, and the Russian-built reactor at Bushehr. He was glad he hadn't drawn that assignment. The team that hit Bushehr might not make it back.

By now, Yossi thought to himself, the prime minister has phoned the White House. No doubt, the Americans will feign shock and displeasure at the plans now set in motion. Yossi smiled. They knew what was coming. And if they did not know in advance, they at least hoped for it. The whole world hoped for Israel to solve their Iranian problem. And now here they were, about to …

A light flashed on the control panel and a tone squawked in the headset. Yossi pressed the microphone. "Target locked."

Pilots from the planes flying with him responded. "Target acquired and locked."

Already in attack formation, the planes rolled to the left and plunged toward the drop zone. Then through the cockpit canopy, the cluster of gray steel buildings came into sight thousands of feet below.

Yossi's thumb was poised to depress the switch that would bring the world to the brink of total destruction…

✧ ✧ ✧

You have just read in this chapter a fictionalized version of an attack on Iran from *Seven Days,* a novel from Mike Evans, of how an attack by Israel against Iran's nuclear sites might be launched. Though these few pages are fiction, the question remains: Would such an attack be the beginning of the end?

COUNT DOWN

I will gather all the nations and bring them
down to the Valley of Jehoshaphat.
And I will enter into judgment with them there,
on behalf of my people and my heritage Israel,
because they have scattered them among
the nations and have divided up my land,...
—JOEL 3:2, ESV

IGNITION

AFTERWORD

·

Solving the Iranian nuclear crisis involves no easy choices. Rather, all decisions have negative consequences. The alternative, then, is to find the best among admittedly less than desirable options. Winning a military invasion of Iran should be easier than winning the peace against Iran. Yet, ironically, removing that oppressive and fanatical regime in Iran might set in motion positive forces throughout the Middle East.

Russia and China, while opposed to any U.S. invasion of Iran, would likely stand aside, deciding not to provide direct military assistance to save the regime of the mullahs, just as they decided to stand by when the United States invaded Iraq to remove Saddam Hussein from power.

Skeptics within the United States and those worldwide will argue that an invasion of Iran would overstretch the U.S. military and prove too costly to undertake. Yet, with U.S. military troops having been withdrawn from Iraq and force levels being reduced in Afghanistan, redeployment to Iran is more achievable now.

Clearly, a military invasion of Iran will not be the option first considered by any U.S. President. At first, removing the regime in Iran will seem too extensive an objective, one not fully demanded by the threat.

Yet, after a serious attempt is made to deal with the Iranian regime on a more limited basis of engagement, a regime-change invasion is the only option that truly makes sense. If our goal is to solve the problem, we might find ourselves frustrated by the Iranian regime's resistance to diplomatic pressure and the ability to absorb an attack on its nuclear facilities without permanently dislodging Iran's nuclear weapons ambition.

Options other than regime-change should be explored first. Still, after months of pursuing more limited objectives and tactical methodologies, the U.S.

may face a fundamental choice: Remove the regime of the mullahs once and for all, or accept the reality that sooner or later the mullahs will end up with nuclear weapons.

Ironically, in the final analysis, what might end up making the most sense is the same solution that we put off with Iraq for over 10 years. After trying everything we could think of short of a regime-changing invasion to rein in Saddam Hussein, we ended up invading simply because we could identify no other solution that had any real hope of long-term success. The same analytics applied to Iran could lead to the same conclusion. The only difference is that with Iran's determined push to develop nuclear weapons, we may not have a decade to explore alternatives.

It should be remembered that Iran has been given an easy solution to the entire crisis: Comply with the IAEA's request for verifiable inspections in conducting a "transparent" nuclear power program aimed 100 percent at civilian purposes.

Perhaps Iran would have to accept Russia's invitation to form a joint venture company under which uranium for Iran could be enriched on Russian soil. Again, if Iran's intentions are entirely peaceful, what is wrong with this compromise? Iranian nuclear scientists and engineers could fully master all the technical issues involved in pursuing the "full fuel cycle."

If Iran wanted to be sure that no one country could deny access to the enriched uranium needed to run a peaceful program, then the IAEA could create a multi-nation "uranium bank" from which Iran could draw the enriched uranium needed on the basis of an internationally guaranteed continuous supply.

The Iranian nuclear crisis can be solved fairly easily and quickly by mature and experienced international diplomats, provided that Iran's intentions are truly peaceful and that Iran would exchange defiance for diplomacy. Too, Iran should also stop attacking Israel with verbal threats and should stop financially supporting terrorist organizations such as Hezbollah.

Yet, the world community would probably step down from crisis mode, as long as Iran's leaders were willing to accept reasonably stated IAEA inspection requirements and nuclear program compromises. Regardless of what the political Left would like to think, the truth is that the last option Israel wants is to solve the Iranian nuclear crisis with an attack. The military option would reflect a failure of sanctions and negotiations, not a victory of the policy pursued by the international community to resolve the nuclear crisis with Iran. And of course, no country wants to draw the U.S., Russia, and China into a Middle East-centered confrontation.

With Israeli-led skirmishes in Syria designed to halt the spread of Iranian arms and war matériel, Russian leader Vladimir Putin shot back a warning to the Israelis that his country would not stand idly by and allow attacks on Bashar al Assad's government in Damascus. Should Russia determine that Syria needed its support, would it be the first step in the battle outlined in Ezekiel 38? Indeed, once it sets a course, Russia appears not to have any recourse:

> "I will turn you around, put hooks into your jaws, and lead you out, with all your army, horses, and horsemen, all splendidly clothed, a great company *with* bucklers and shields, all of them handling swords," (Ezekiel 38:4).

What will be the outcome of Russia's headlong rush towards Israel:

> "I will call for a sword against Gog throughout all My mountains," says the Lord GOD. "Every man's sword will be against his brother. And I will bring him to judgment with pestilence and bloodshed; I will rain down on him, on his troops, and on the many peoples who *are* with him, flooding rain, great hailstones, fire, and brimstone," (Ezekiel 38:21-22).

Israel is heir to the same promise made to Abraham in Genesis 12:3:

> "I will bless those who bless you, And I will **curse him who curses you**; And in you all the families of the earth shall be blessed." (Emphasis mine.)

Or as the prophet Zechariah wrote in chapter 2, verse 8 (NKJV), "...for he who touches you touches the apple of His eye." The New International Version paints an even more comforting picture, "For He said, 'Anyone who harms you harms my most precious possession.'"

ENDNOTES

1. Yossi Melman, Meir Javedanfar, *The Nuclear Sphinx of Tehran,* (New York, NY: Basic Books, 2008), pp.89–90.

2. Fitzpatrick, Mark (2007). "§*Dr. A. Q. Khan and the rise and fall of proliferation network". Nuclear black markets.* London, United Kingdom: International Institute for Strategic Studies (IISS).

3. Ibid.

4. "Rafsanjani Says Muslims Should Use Nuclear Weapon Against Israel," Iran Press Service, December 14, 2001, http://www.iran-press-service.com/articles_2001/dec_2001/rafsanjani_nuke_threats_141201.htm; accessed March 2013.

5. Ibid.

6. Carla Anne Robbins, "North Korea Got a Little Help from Neighbors—Secret Nuclear Program Tapped Russian Suppliers and Pakistani Know-How," *Wall Street Journal Europe,* October 21, 2002; ABC's *This Week,* October 20, 2002 (transcript).

7. David E. Sanger and William J. Broad, "From Rogue Nuclear Programs, Web of Trails Leads to Pakistan," *New York Times,* January 4, 2004, http://select.nytimes.com/gst/abstract.html?res=F00B16FC3F550C778CDDA808 94DC404482; accessed November 10, 2004.

8. Joby Warrick, "Nuclear Program in Iran Tied to Pakistan; Complex Network Acquired Technology and Blueprints," *The Washington Post* (December 21, 2003), A.01.

9. Paul Leventhal, "Testimony before the House Committee on International Relations Subcommittee on the Middle East and Central Asia hearing on 'Iranian Proliferation: Implications for Terrorists, Their State Sponsors, and US Countermeasures,'" June 24, 2004.

10. "Abdul Qadeer Kahn 'Apologizes' for Transferring Nuclear Secrets Abroad." The statement is archived on the Federation of American Scientists website, www.fas.org, at the following URL: http://www.fas.org/nuke/guide/ pakistan/nuke/aqkhan020404.html.

11. Vice-President Dick Cheney vs. John Edwards, "2004 Vice-Presidential Debate," *Commission on Presidential Debates,* http://www.debates.org/pages/trans2004b.html; accessed December 12, 2006.

12. Report by the Director General, International Atomic Energy Agency (IAEA), "Implementation of the NPT Safeguards Agreement in the Islamic Republic of Iran," GOV/2005/87, November 18, 2005. http://www. globalsecurity.org/wmd/library/report/2005/iran_iaea_gov2005-87_18nov05.pdf

13. "Dr. Abdul Qadeer Khan," http://www.forumpakistan.com/dr-abdul-qadeer-khan-t3919.html; accessed March 2013.

14. James Risen, "State of War: The Secret History of the CIA and the Bush Administration," *Free Press,* January 2006.

15. On *GlobalSecurity.org*. This Internet site contains an extensive discussion of Iran's nuclear facilities, including a site-by-site description, reached by navigating through the following sequence: Iran > Facilities > Nuclear. The discussion of Iran's uranium mines is drawn from this site: http://www.globalsecurity.org/wmd/world/ iran/mines.htm; accessed 2006.

16. Saghand Mining Department, Atomic Energy Organization of Iran. http://www.aeoi.org.ir/NewWeb/Recenter. asp?id=26 See also: National Geoscience Database of Iran (NGDIR), "Mineral Resources of Iran." http://ngdir. ir/GeoportalInfo/SubjectInfoDetail.asp?PID=54&index=67; accessed 2006.

17. "AP: Iran to Extract Uranium in Early 2006," News Max wires, at *NewsMax.com* September 6, 2004. http:// www.newsmax.com/archives/articles/2004/9/5/115634.shtml; accessed 2005.

18. "Esfahan/Isfahan. Nuclear Technology," *GlobalSecurity.org*, at: http://www.globalsecurity.org/wmd/world/iran/ esfahan.htm; accessed 2006.

19. "Revealed: Iran's Nuclear Factory," *The Sunday Times-World,* May 1, 2005, archived at *Timesonline.co.uk* at: http://www.timesonline.co.uk/article/0,,2089-1592578,00.html; accessed 2005.

20. "Natanz," at *GlobalSecurity.org.* http://www.globalsecurity.org/wmd/world/iran/natanz.htm

21. "EU powers to mull Iranian nuclear efforts," *Haaretz,* February 9, 2004. http://www.haaretz.com/hasen/pages/ ShArt.jhtml?itemNo=472862&contrassID=1; accessed 2006.

22. "Iran confirms uranium-to-gas conversion," a report published in the *China Daily,* May 10, 2005. http://www. chinadaily.com.cn/english/doc/2005-05/10/content_440631.htm

23. Ibid.

24. Tom Baldwin, "Iran faces sanctions after reactivating nuclear plant," *TimesOnLine.com,* August 9, 2005. http://www.timesonline.co.uk/article/0,,251-1727066,00.html See also: Seth Rosen, "Iran restarts its nuclear activities," The Washington Times, August 9, 2005. http://www.washtimes.com/world/20050809-120112- 3017r.htm; accessed 2006.

25. "Iran Rejects U.N. Resolution," CBS News, September 25, 2005. http://www.cbsnews.com/stories/2005/09/25/ world/main882946.shtml. (Accessed 2006)

26. *Reuters*, "Iran enriches uranium. Iran starts converting new uranium batch, diplomat says," November 27, 2005. http://www.blog.ca/main/index.php/borisnewz/2005/11/17/iran_enriches_uranium~315692. (Accessed 2006)

27. *Reuters*, "Russia plan could end Iran talks impasse—ElBaradei," December 6, 2005. http://today.reuters.co.uk/news/newsArticle.aspx?type=worldNews&storyID=2005-12-06T173520Z_01_DIT663295_RTRUKOC_0_UK-NUCLEAR-IRAN-ELBARADEI.xml; accessed 2006.

28. Information provided by the National Council of Resistance of Iran, U.S. Representative Office. "Information on Two Top Secret Nuclear Sites of the Iranian Regime (Natanz and Arak)," December 2002. The Report is available on the website *IranWatch.org* at the URL: http://www.iranwatch.org/privateviews/NCRI/perspex-ncri-natanzarak-1202.htm; accessed 2006.

29. National Council for Resistance in Iran, "Disclosing a Major Secret Nuclear Site under the Ministry of Defense," Press Release, November 14, 2004. Archived on the website of *GlobalSecurity.org* at: http://www.globalsecurity.org/wmd/library/report/2004/new-nuke-info.htm; accessed 2006.

30. "Implementation of the NPT Safeguards Agreement in the Islamic Republic of Iran," Report by the Director General, International Atomic Energy Agency (IAEA) Board of Governors, GOV/2006/67, September 2, 2005. http://www.globalsecurity.org/wmd/library/report/2005/iran_iaea-gov_2005-67_2sep05.htm; accessed 2006.

31. "Questioning Iran's Pursuit of the Nuclear Fuel Cycle—Iran's Nuclear Fuel Cycle Facilities: A Pattern of Peaceful Intent?" U.S. Department of State, September 2005. http://www.globalsecurity.org/wmd/library/report/2005/iran-fuel-cycle-brief_dos_2005.pdf; accessed 2006.

32. Ibid.

33. Ibid.

34. Ibid.

35. Ibid.

36. Ibid.

37. Attachment A, Unclassified Report to Congress on the Acquisition of Technology Relating to Weapons of Mass Destruction and Advanced Conventional Munitions, 1 July through 31 December 2003. The report can be found on the Internet on the website of the Central Intelligence Agency at the following URL: http://www.cia.gov/cia/reports/721_reports/july_dec2003.htm; accessed 2005.

38. Ibid.

39. "Iran Claims Solid Fuel for Missiles Achieved," *NewsMax.com*, July 27, 2005. http://www.newsmax.com/archives/articles/2005/7/27/104439.shtml, (Accessed 2006)

40. Anthony H. Cordesman, Arleigh A. Burke Chair, Center for Strategic and International Studies, *Iran's Developing Military Capabilities: Main Report* Washington, D.C. Center for Strategic and International Studies; Working Draft: December 14, 2004. The discussion of the *Shahab*-3 missile is drawn from pages 25-27.

41. "Nuclear Weapons development—2006," Global Security.org, http://www.globalsecurity.org/wmd/world/iran/nuke2006.htm; accessed July 2009.

42. "Iran's nuclear program status," Congressional Research Service, November 20, 2008; p. CRS-10, http://www.fas.org/sgp/crs/nuke/RL34544.pdf; accessed July 2009.

43. HR282, Iran Freedom Support Act, U.S. House bill, April 27, 2006. http://www.theorator.com/bills109/hr282.html; accessed July 2009.

44. Dudi Cohen, "Israel will soon disappear," *Ynetnews*, October 10, 2006, http://www.ynetnews.com/articles/0,7340,L-3317417,00.html; accessed July 2009.

45. Michael Goldfarb, editor, "Ahmadinejad: World has lost its will," *Weekly Standard*, November 14, 2006; http://www.weeklystandard.com/weblogs/TWSFP/2006/11/ahmadinejad_world_has_lost_its_will_.html; accessed July 2009.

46. "Iran determined to master nuclear fuel cycle," *Iran Daily*, November 15, 2006; http://iran-daily.com/1385/2708/html/index.htm. (Accessed July 2009)

47. "Key judgements from a National Intelligence Estimate on Iran's nuclear activity," *The New York Times*, December 4, 2007; http://www.nytimes.com/2007/12/04/washington/04itext.html?pagewanted=2&_r=2; accessed July 2009.

48. David Albright and Jacqueline Shire, "IAEA Report on Iran," Institute for Science and International Security, 19 February 2009.

49. James Hider, "Middle East desire for nuclear power could trigger an arms race," Times Online, June 24, 2009, http://www.timesonline.co.uk/tol/news/world/middle_east/article6565549.ece#cid=OTC-RSS&attr=797093; accessed July 2009.

50. "IAEA: Iran broke law by failing to disclose nuclear facility," *Ynet News*, 30 September 2009; accessed July 2010.

51. Personal interview, Mike Evans with Lt. Gen. Moshe Ya'alon in Israel, 2010.

52. Hooman Majd, *The Ayatollah Begs to Differ : The Paradox of Modern Iran*, (New York, NY: Doubleday, 2008), p.84-5

53. George Jahn (28 November 2009). "Nuclear agency comes down on Iran". *Associated Press* via *The Raleigh News & Observer.*

54. Joby Warrick and Scott Wilson (19 February 2010). "Iran might be seeking to develop nuclear weapons capability, inspectors say," *Washington Post.*

55. Julian Borger, diplomatic editor. "European states call for stiffer sanctions against Iran following IAEA report," *Guardian*. http://www.guardian.co.uk/world/2011/nov/09/calls-tougher-sanctions-iran-iaea?newsfeed=true; accessed April 2012.

56. "IAEA resolution to sharply criticize Iran for nuclear efforts," *Washington Post*, November 2011; accessed November 2011.

57. "New claims emerge involving scientist in Iran nuke report". *Usatoday.com*. http://www.usatoday.com/news/world/story/2011-11-11/iran-nuclear-weapons-soviet-scientist/51166144/1; accessed April 2012.

58. Radio Free Europe, "IAEA seeks Parchin Access; Iran says No, January 15, 2013, http://www.rferl.org/content/iaea-iran-parchin-access/24824662.html; accessed January 2013.

59. Fredrik Dahl (28 February 2012), "Iran may be "struggling" with new nuclear machines," *Reuters*; accessed March 2011.

60. "Russia, China join West in Iran rebuke at U.N. nuclear meet," *Reuters*; September 13, 2012; accessed September 2012.

61. Shashank Bengali, "IAEA reports no progress on access to Iran's nuclear facilities, *Los Angeles Times*, December 7, 2012. http://articles.latimes.com/2012/dec/07/world/la-fg-iran-nuclear-20121207; accessed December 2012.

62. Joel Gehrke, "Netanyahu reminds Obama that his diplomacy isn't thwarting Iran's nuclear program," Washington Examiner, March 13, 2013, http://washingtonexaminer.com/netanyahu-reminds-obama-that-his-diplomacy-isnt-thwarting-irans-nuclear-program/article/2524924; accessed March 2013.

63. David Albright and Christina Walrond, "North Korea's Estimated Stocks of Plutonium and Weapon-Grade Uranium, http://isis-online.org/uploads/isis-reports/documents/dprk_fissile_material_production_16Aug2012.pdf, page 10; accessed April 2013.

64. "Iran sent 50,000 missiles to Gaza," http://www.memri.org/report/en/0/0/0/0/108/0/7160.htm; accessed May 2013.

65. Ibid.

66. "Ahmadinejad and the Mahdi," *Hyscience*, May 5, 2005, http://www.hyscience.com/archives/2006/05/ahmadinejad_and.php (accessed December 14, 2006).

67. Raymond Tanter, personal interview with Mike Evans, June 15, 2006.

68. http://www.shoebat.com/. Accessed May 2010.

69. John R. Bolton, "Iran's Continuing Pursuit of Weapons of Mass Destruction," Testimony Before the House International Relations Committee Subcommittee on the Middle East and Central Asia, June 24, 2005, http://www.state.gov/t/us/rm/33909.htm; accessed December 2006.

70. "Ayatollah Ali Khamenei says Iran, Israel on 'collision course'", Ramin Mostaghim and Borzou Daragahi, *Los Angeles Times*, September 20, 2008; http://articles.latimes.com/2008/sep/20/world/fg-iran20. (Accessed July 2009)

71. Patrick Devenny "Hezbollah's strategic threat to Israel," *Middle East Quarterly*, Winter 2006, pp. 31-38; http://www.meforum.org/806/hezbollahs-strategic-threat-to-israel. (Accessed July 2009)

72. Foreign Broadcast Information Service - Daily Reports, July 20, 1994; Source—*Radio Iran*; Quoted in "The Islamic Republic of Iran and the Holocaust: Anti-Semitism and Anti-Zionism," Meir Litvak, *The Journal of Israeli History*, V. 25, No. 1, March 2006, PP. 267-284, 271.

73. Comment by Mahmoud Ahmadinejad, March 1, 2007, Quoted in "Zionist regime offspring of Britain, nurtured by US—Ahmadinejad," *Islamic Republic News Agency* (IRNA), http://www2.irna.ir/en/news/view/line-20/0703015352005938.htm. (Accessed July 2009)

74. Personal interview with Benjamin Netanyahu, 2007.

75. Ibid.

76. David Ignatius, "The Spy who wants Israel to talk," *Washington Post*, November 11, 2007; http://www.washingtonpost.com/wp-dyn/content/article/2007/11/09/AR2007110901941.html; accessed July 2009.

77. Mahmoud Ahmadinejad, United Nations, September 17, 2005 speech; http://www.globalsecurity.org/wmd/library/news/iran/2005/iran-050918-irna02.htm; accessed July 2009.

78. Golnaz Esfandiari, "Iran: President Says Light Surrounded Him During UN Speech," Radio Free Europe/Radio Liberty, November 29, 2005. http://www.rferl.org/featuresarticle/2005/11/184CB9FB-887C-4696-8F54-0799DF747A4A.html *RegimeChangeIran.blogspot.com* provides a link to a news broadcast where the videotape of Ahmadinejad's conversations with the mullahs over tea can be seen and heard: http://regimechangeiran.blogspot.com/2005/12/important-video-report-on-hidden-iman.html See also, Scott Peterson, "Waiting for the rapture in Iran," *Christian Science Monitor*, 21 December 2005.

79. "Iran: Part of the Axis of Evil," April 22, 2006; http://www.zionism-israel.com/log/archives/00000042.html; accessed July 2009.

80. LookLex Encyclopedia, "Twelvers", http://i-cias.com/e.o/twelvers.htm; accessed July 2009.

81. Jamie Glazov, "The China-Russia-Iran Axis", *FrontPageMagazine*.com, January 22, 2008, http://www.frontpagemag.com/readArticle.aspx?ARTID=29604; accessed August 2009.

82. Trudy Rubin, "Hold Off Engaging Iran," *Miami Herald*, July 23, 2009; http://www.miamiherald.com/opinion/other-views/v-fullstory/story/1153627.html; accessed August 2009.

83. "What is Globalization?" http://www.globalization101.org/What_is_Globalization.html?PHPSESSID=e54636b5a846c31e34b20315060d2a71; accessed August 2009.

84. Benjamin Netanyahu, Translation, Prime Minister's Office, July 28, 2009; http://www.pmo.gov.il/PMOEng/Communication/PMSpeaks/speechmabal280709.htm; accessed August 2009.

85. Jim Kingsdale's Energy Investment Strategies, "Iranian oil production verging on disaster," June 2008; http://www.energyinvestmentstrategies.com/2008/06/25/iranian-oil-production-verging-on-disaster/; accessed August 2009.

86. "Iran to end petrol import," Press TV, August 1, 2009; http://www.presstv.com/detail.aspx?id=102237&sectionid=351020102; accessed August 2009.

87. Avner Cohen, Israel and the Bomb (New York, NY: Columbia University Press, 1998), p. 135.

88. George Perkovich, "The Sampson Option," February 19, 2006, Carnegie Endowment for International Peace, http://www.carnegieendowment.org/2006/02/19/sampson-option/1o04; accessed March 2013.

89. The Phrase Finder, http://www.phrases.org.uk/bulletin_board/60/messages/716.html; accessed March 2013.

90. Joe Holley, "Counsel to Kennedy, Myer Feldman; Vital to Special Olympics," *Washington Post*, Post Morten, http://www.washingtonpost.com/wp-dyn/content/article/2007/03/02/AR2007030201764.html; accessed March 2013.

91. George Perkovich, reviewer, *The Samson Option, The Washington Post*, February 19, 2006, http://www.washingtonpost.com/wp-dyn/content/article/2006/02/16/AR2006021601897.html; accessed March 2013.

92. http://www.brainyquote.com/quotes/quotes/g/goldameir137486.html#UzdJe42wRXzu2E5r.99; accessed March 2013.

93. Seymour M. Hersh, *The Price of Power: Kissinger in the Nixon White House* (New York: Summit Books, 1983), p. 234.

94. Jason Maoz, "Nixon: The Anti-Semite who Saved Israel," *The Jewish Press*, August 5, 2005.

95. Keith Koffler, "Obama Wildly Cheered by Reform Jews," December 16, 2011, *white house dossier*; http://www.whitehousedossier.com/2011/12/16/obama-wildly-cheered-reform-jews/; accessed January 2012.

96. "Zionism, Nixon-style," *The Jerusalem Post* editorial, December 12, 2010; http://www.jpost.com/Opinion/Editorials/Article.aspx?id=199133&R=R6; accessed January 2012.

97. Robert S. Norris, William Arkin, Hans M. Kristensen, and Joshua Handler (September/October 2002), "Israeli nuclear forces, 2002", *Bulletin of the Atomic Scientists* 58, Volume 5, pp. 73–5.

98. Kenneth S. Brower, "A Propensity for Conflict: Potential Scenarios and Outcomes of War in the Middle East", February 1997, *Jane's Intelligence Review*, Volume 14, pp. 14–5.

99. Douglas Frantz,(Sunday, October 12, 2003), "Israel Adds Fuel to Nuclear Dispute, Officials confirm that the nation can now launch atomic weapons from land, sea and air", *The Los Angeles Times*, October 12, 2003, http://www.commondreams.org/headlines03/1012-02.htm; accessed March 2013.

100. Martin Van Creveld, *The Culture of War*, (New York, NY: Random House Digital, 2008), p. 284.

101. Yaakov Katz, "Mum's the N-word". *The Jerusalem Post*, December 15, 2006, p. 14.

102. Alvah Bessie, Brainy Quotes, Canary Quotes, http://www.brainyquote.com/quotes/keywords/canary.html#WBVt0uPKZhJX8tXM.99; accessed April 2013.

103. Muslim Brother Motto, http://www.usmessageboard.com/politics/153351-muslim-brotherhood-in-the-usa.html; accessed April 2013.

104. "Jordan Islamists vow to continue protests until reforms adopted," *M & C*, March 10, 2011; http://www.monstersandcritics.com/news/middleeast/news/article_1625064.php/Jordan-Islamists-vow-to-continue-protests-until-reforms-adopted; accessed March 2011.

105. Rafael D. Frankel, "Why Israel May Go it Alone," *The National Interest*, October 5, 2012, http://nationalinterest.org/commentary/will-israel-go-it-alone-7538; accessed April 2013.

106. Jeffrey Heller, "US Has no Right to Block Israel on Iran: Netanyahu," http://www.reuters.com/article/2012/09/11/us-israel-iran-netanyahu-idUSBRE88A0FO20120911; accessed April 2013.

107. "U.S. Favorability Ratings Remain Positive: China Seen Overtaking U.S. as Global Superpower," Pew Research Global Attitudes Project, July 13, 2011, http://www.pewglobal.org/2011/07/13/china-seen-overtaking-us-as-global-superpower/; accessed April 2013.

108. Jeffrey Goldberg, "Obama to Iran and Israel, 'As President of the United States, I don't bluff,'" The Atlantic, March 2, 2012, http://www.theatlantic.com/international/archive/2012/03/obama-to-iran-and-israel-as-president-of-the-united-states-i-dont-bluff/253875/; accessed April 2013.

109. James Earl Carter, Jr., State of the Union Address 1981; http://www.let.rug.nl/usa/P/jc39/speeches/su81jec.htm; accessed February 2008.

110. Bret Stephens, "How to Stop Iran without Firing a Shot"; May 15, 2006; http://www.opinionjournal.com/wsj/?id=110008382; accessed February, 2008.

111. "Obama holding talks with Iran excluding Israel," The Jerusalem Post, December 11, 2012, http://www.jpost.com/IranianThreat/News/Article.aspx?id=295560; accessed December 2012.

112. "Iran congratulates North Korea on rocket launch," YahooNews, December 12, 2012, http://uk.news.yahoo.com/iran-congratulates-north-korea-rocket-launch-145452352.html; accessed December 2012.

113. Dante Alighieri, http://thinkexist.com/quotation/the_hottest_places_in_hell_are_reserved_for_those/169930.html; accessed December 2012.

114. "Arabs like Saddam, Hugo Chavez, more than Obama," December 13, 2012, http://educationviews.org/arabs-like-saddam-hugo-chavez-more-than-obama/; accessed December 2012.

115. List of Current ships of the US Navy, http://en.wikipedia.org/wiki/List_of_current_ships_of_the_United_States_Navy; accessed October 2012.

116. Websites of the military installations discussed are as follows: Ft. Rucker, Alabama, at http://www-rucker.army.mil ; Hulburt Field, Florida http://www.hurlburt.af.mil/index2.shtml ; http://www.29palms.usmc.mil/ The authors are acknowledge an unpublished paper by Paul L. Williams, "U.S. Invasion of Iran Now 'Imminent,'" as identifying the importance of these bases in preparing for a U.S. military attack on Iran.

117. Iran's nuclear facilities are detailed at GlobalSecurity.org, including in many instances satellite photographs. http://www.globalsecurity.org/wmd/world/iran/nuke-fac.htm

118. NTI, "Iran Profile: Iran Missile Facilities," NTI.org, at the following URL: http://www.nti.org/e_research/profiles/Iran/Missile/3876_4104.html

119. See, for Instance, Global Security.org at the following URL: http://www.globalsecurity.org/military/world/iran/

120. Robert Coram, Boyd: The Fighter Pilot Who Changed the Art of War (Boston: Little, Brown and Company, 2002), page 42.

121. Described in Bijal Trivedi, "Inside Shock and Awe," National Geographic Channel, posted to the website on Feb. 14, 2005, at the following URL: http://blogs.nationalgeographic.com/channel/blog/2005/03/explorer_shockawe.html

122. Robert Tait, "Iran issues stark warning on oil price," The Guardian, Jan. 16, 2006. http://www.guardian.co.uk/frontpage/story/0,16518,1687381,00.html

123. For a technical description of the Eros B satellite, see: ImageSat International, Owners and Operators of the EROS Family, at: http://www.imagesatintl.com/?catid=%7B0CD18AE4-F495-420A-A0FF-3D5A4512020B%7D

124. Associated Press, "Israeli spy satellite launched to watch Iran," April 25, 2006. Posted on MSNBC.com at the following Internet address: http://www.msnbc.msn.com/id/12481685/

125. "Interview with Yitzhak Ben Yisreal, Head of the Israeli Space Agency, Discussing the New Israeli Satellite to Spy on the Iranian Nuclear Program," TMCnet.com, April 26, 2006. http://www.tmcnet.com/usubmit/-interview-with-yitzhak-ben-yisrael-head-the-israeli-/2006/04/27/1617119.htm

126. "President Bush's speech of 8/31/2006," Georgewbush-whitehouse.archives.gov, August 31, 2006; accessed September 2012.

127. "Iran's Nuclear Program," 1913 Intel.com, http://www.1913intel.com/2007/07/10/irans-nuclear-program/; accessed April 2013.

128. "Bush: Iran's defiance will bring 'consequences'", August 31, 2006, CNN, Lou Dobbs Tonight, http://transcripts.cnn.com/TRANSCRIPTS/0608/31/ldt.01.html; accessed April 2013.

129. Seymour Hersh, "Hersh: U.S. mulls nuclear option for Iran," CNN, April 10, 2006, accessed February 2008.

130. "Iran Shuns US Carrot-with-stick," BBC News, December 8, 2008, http://news.bbc.co.uk/2/hi/7771821.stm; accessed April 2013.

131. Obama: Iranian threats against Israel 'unacceptable', Jewish Telegraphic Agency (JTA), December 7, 2008; accessed April 2013..

132. "The White House: Foreign Policy," Whitehouse.gov; accessed September 2009.

133. "Mr. Obama and Iran," Editorial, New York Times, February 8, 2009, http://www.nytimes.com/2009/02/09/opinion/09mon1.html?_r=0; accessed April 2009.

134. "Iran's first nuclear plant begins Fueling," CNN, August 21, 2010; accessed August 2010.

135. Tabassum Zakaria, "Iran could reach key point for nuclear bomb by mid-2014: U.S. experts," Reuters; accessed January 2013.

136. Sir Winston Churchill, http://quotes.liberty-tree.ca/quote/winston_churchill_quote_1c74; accessed April 2013.

137. Brian Murphy, "Ayatollah Ali Khamenei, Iran Supreme Leader, Scolds Ahmadinejad ahead of Elections," *Huffington Post*, February 17, 2013, http://www.huffingtonpost.com/2013/02/17/ayatollah-ali-khamenei-ahmadinejad_n_2707814.html; accessed May 2013.

138. Henry Wadsworth Longfellow, "Paul Revere's Ride," http://poetry.eserver.org/paul-revere.html; accessed April 2013.

139. Rafael Eitan, "The Raid on the Reactor from the Point of View of the Chief of Staff," *Israel's Strike against the Iraqi Nuclear Reactor 7 June, 1981*, Jerusalem: Menachem Begin Heritage Center: 2003, 31-33.

140. Maj. Gen. (res.) David Ivry, "The Attack on the Osiraq Nuclear Reactor—Looking Back 21 Years Later," *Israel's Strike against the Iraqi Nuclear Reactor 7 June, 1981*, Jerusalem: Menachem Begin Heritage Center, 2003, p. 35.

141. Yitzhak Shamir, "The Failure of Diplomacy," *Israel's Strike Against the Iraqi Nuclear Reactor 7 June, 1981*, Jerusalem, Menachem Begin Heritage Center: 2003, p. 16-17.

142. "Bush: North Korea Defies International Community," *CNN.com*, http://www.cnn.com/2006/POLITICS/10/09/bush.korea.transcript/index.html; accessed April 2013.

143. Ibid.

144. "The Future of the U.S. Military and Irregular Warfare," Center for Strategic and International Studies, November 22, 2005, http://csis.org/event/future-us-military-and-irregular-warfare; accessed April 2013.

145. David A. Fulghum, "U.S. Electronic Surveillance Monitored Israeli Attack On Syria", *Aviation Week & Space Technology*, November 11, 2007; accessed April 2013.

146. Conal Urquhart, "Speculation flourishes over Israel's strike on Syria", *The Guardian*, September 17, 2007; accessed April 2013.

147. "Israel Unveils World's Largest UAV," Homeland Security News Wire, http://www.homelandsecuritynewswire.com/israel-unveils-worlds-largest-uav; February 20, 2010; accessed April 2013.

148. "Israel Eyes Azerbaijan for raid on Iran," UPI.com, December 3, 2012, http://www.upi.com/Top_News/Special/2012/12/03/Israel-eyes-Azerbaijan-for-raid-on-Iran/UPI-74411354572297/; accessed April 2013.

149. Thom Shanker and David Sanger, "U.S. Suspects Iran was Behind a Wave of Cyberattacks," *The New York Times*, October 13, 2012, http://www.nytimes.com/2012/10/14/world/middleeast/us-suspects-iranians-were-behind-a-wave-of-cyberattacks.html?pagewanted=all&_r=0; accessed May 2013.

150. Robert McMillan, "Was Stuxnet Built to Attack Iran's Nuclear Program," *PC World,* September 21, 2010, http://www.pcworld.com/article/205827/was_stuxnet_built_to_attack_irans_nuclear_program.html; accessed April 2013.

151. Ibid.

152. "Full Analysis of Flame's Command and Control Servers," http://www.securelist.com/en/blog/750/Full_Analysis_of_Flames_Command_Control_servers; accessed May 2013.

153. Peter Beaumont, "Cyber war on Iran more widespread than first thought, say researchers," *The Guardian*, September 21, 2012, http://www.guardian.co.uk/technology/2012/sep/21/cyberwar-iran-more-sophisticated; accessed May 2013.

154. BBC News, "U.S. to sell bunker bombs to Israel, April 28, 2005, http://news.bbc.co.uk/2/hi/middle_east/4493443.stm

155. Eli Lake, "Obama Sold Israel Bunker-Buster Bombs," September 23, 2011, The Daily Beast, http://www.thedailybeast.com/articles/2011/09/23/president-obama-secretly-approved-transfer-of-bunker-buster-bombs-to-israel.html; accessed April 2013.

156. "Guided Bomb Unit-28 (GBU-28)," GlobalSecurity.org, at the following URL: http://www.globalsecurity.org/military/systems/munitions/gbu-28.htm This site includes technical specifications and photographs of the GBU-28.

157. All Military Weapons.com, http://www.allmilitaryweapons.com/2011/02/jericho-ii-and-iii-israeli-ballistic.html; accessed April 2013.

158. For technical descriptions and photographs of the Popeye Turbo cruise missile, see: "Popeye Turbo," on the website *IsraeliWeapons.com*. http://www.israeli-weapons.com/weapons/missile_systems/air_missiles/popeye_turbo/Popeye_Turbo.html; accessed January 2013.

159. "F-16I Soufa fighter and Ground Attack Aircraft, Israel," featured on the website of Airforce-Technology.com at the following URL: http://www.airforce-technology.com/projects/f-16i/ In addition to technical specifications, the website also has photographs of the F-16I.

160. For technical specifications and photographs of the F-16I, see Israeli-Weapons.com at the following URL: http://www.israeli-weapons.com/weapons/aircraft/f-15i/F-15I.html This site also provides technical specifications and photographs for the F-16I at http://www.israeli-weapons.com/weapons/aircraft/f-16i/F-16I.html

161. John Hudson, "The Playbook for an Israeli Airstrike on Iran's Nuclear Facilities," *The Atlantic Wire*, February 21, 2012, http://www.theatlanticwire.com/global/2012/02/playbook-israeli-airstrike-irans-nuclear-facilities/48945/; accessed April 2013.

162. Dr. Scott Firsing, "Israel vs. Iran Fight Breakdown," Foreign Policy Association, December 13, 2011, http://foreignpolicyblogs.com/2011/12/13/israel-vs-iran-fight-breakdown/; accessed April 2013.

163. Jim Michaels, "Israeli Attack on Iran would be Complex Operation," *USAToday*, February 13, 2012, http://usatoday30.usatoday.com/news/world/story/2012-02-13/israel-iran-attack/53083160/1; accessed May 2013.

164. INS Dakar, http://en.wikipedia.org/wiki/INS_Dakar; accessed May 2013.

165. Ben Norman, "The mystery of the 'Dakar'," *The Jerusalem Post*, May 27, 2009, http://www.jpost.com/Magazine/Features/The-mystery-of-the-Dakar; accessed May 2013.

166. "The Battle of Latakia," October 7, 1973, http://www.jewishvirtuallibrary.org/jsource/History/latakia.html; accessed May 2013.

167. Yom Kippur War, http://en.wikipedia.org/wiki/Yom_Kippur_war; accessed May 2013.

168. William Shakespeare, *Hamlet*, http://www.allgreatquotes.com/sea_quotes.shtml ; accessed April 2013.

169. Tia Goldenberg, "Israel gets 4th nuke-capable German submarine," May 3, 2012, http://www.boston.com/business/articles/2012/05/03/israel_gets_fourth_german_submarine/; accessed April 2013.

170. Edmund Sanders, "Israel aims to become region's undisputed naval power," *Gulfnews.com*, May 12, 2013, http://gulfnews.com/news/region/palestinian-territories/israel-aims-to-become-region-s-undisputed-naval-power-1.1021995; accessed April 2013.

171. Warda Al-Jawahiry, "U.S. Navy:Iran Prepares Suicide bomb Boats in the Gulf," February 13, 2012, http://www.reuters.com/article/2012/02/13/us-gulf-usa-iran-idUSTRE81B0V220120213; accessed April 2013.

172. U.S. Military Testing a Missile-armed, remote-controlled robotic boats, http://www.allmilitaryweapons.com/2012/10/us-military-testing-missile-armed.html; accessed April 2013.

173. "Israeli Navy Revamps for Hybrid, Littoral, and Strategic Warfare," Offiziere.ch,

174. "21st CENTURY FRIGATES TODAY," G2mil.com, http://www.g2mil.com/frigate.htm; accessed November 2012.

175. Leo Rennert, "Israel Strengthens Nuclear Deterrent Against Iran with Fleet of German Subs," February 6, 2012, http://www.americanthinker.com/blog/2012/02/israel_strengthens_nuclear_deterrent_against_iran_with_fleet_of_german_subs.html#ixzz2RD2iPN2P; accessed April 2013.

176. Robert Burns, "Hagel stresses Israel's right to strike Iran," *Yahoo News*, April 21, 2013, http://news.yahoo.com/hagel-stresses-israels-strike-iran-161831505--politics.html; accessed April 2013.

177. Ibid.

178. "Iran: President Ahmadinejad unveils new fighter jet," http://www.jpost.com/Iranian-Threat/News/Iran-President-Ahmadinejad-unveils-new-fighter-jet; accessed April 2013.

179. Elizabeth Bumiller, "Iran Raid seen as a Huge Task for Israeli Jets," The New York Times, February 19, 2012, http://www.nytimes.com/2012/02/20/world/middleeast/iran-raid-seen-as-complex-task-for-israeli-military.html?pagewanted=1&_r=1&; accessed April 2013.

180. Ibid.

181. Current Concerns, March 19, 2012, http://www.currentconcerns.ch/index.php?id=1657; accessed April 2013.

182. Ibid.

183. Ibid.

184. Michael Elleman, "Everything You Wanted to Know About Iran's Air Force," March 12, 2013, http://www.realclearworld.com/articles/2013/03/12/everything_you_wanted_to_know_about_irans_air_force_100613.html; accessed April 2013.

185. Charles Swindoll, "The Shadow of the Giant, Part I," May 13, 2009, http://daily.insight.org/site/News2?page=NewsArticle&id=14179; accessed April 2013.

186. Michael Elleman, "Everything You Wanted to Know About Iran's Air Force," March 12, 2013, http://www.realclearworld.com/articles/2013/03/12/everything_you_wanted_to_know_about_irans_air_force_100613.html; accessed April 2013.

187. Radio Free Europe, Iran: Unemployment becoming a 'National Threat,'" April 25, 2013, http://www.rferl.org/content/article/1051866.html; accessed April 2013.

188. Kenneth M. Pollock and Ray Takeyh, "Taking on Tehran," March/April 2005, Council on Foreign Relations, http://www.cfr.org/world/taking-tehran/p8067; accessed November 2012.

189. "Sanctions begin to Bite," *Economist*, October 2010 edition, http://www.economist.com/node/17204603; accessed December 2012.

190. Council on Foreign Relations, "Iran's Nuclear Program Symposium: Iran's Motives and Strategy" [Rush Transcript; Federal News Service, Inc.], http://www.cfr.org/iran/irans-nuclear-program-symposium-irans-motives-strategy-rush-transcript-federal-news-service-inc/p10389; accessed April 2013.

191. Financial Times Enforcement Network, USA Patriot Act, Section 311, http://www.fincen.gov/statutes_regs/patriot/section311.html; accessed August 2009.

192. David Ignatius, "U.S. Sanctions with Teeth," *Washington Post,* February 29, 2007; http://washingtonpost.com/wp-dyn/content/article/2007/02/07/27/AR2007022701157_p; accessed July 2009.

193. Stuart E. Eizenstat, "Mega-Trends in the Next Five Years Which Will Impact on World Jewry and Israel," Conference on the Future of the Jewish People, May 2008, Jerusalem Israel; The Jewish People Policy Planning Institute, http://www.jpppi.org.il/JPPPI/Templates/ShowPage.asp?DBID=1&LNGID=1&TMID=105&FID=452&PID=0&IID=510. pp. 67-68; accessed August 2009.

194. Jonathan Saul, "Iran parks millions of oil barrels on tankers as buyers retreat," April 24, 2013 http://www.reuters.com/article/2013/04/24/us-iran-shipping-oil-idUSBRE93N0XX20130424, accessed May 2013.

195. "Sanctions reduced Iran's oil exports and revenues in 2012," US Energy Information Administration, April 26, 2013, http://www.eia.gov/todayinenergy/detail.cfm?id=11011; accessed May 2013.

196. Javier Blas, "New oil sanctions start to bite Iran," *Financial Times*, April 30, 2013,http://www.ft.com/intl/cms/s/0/f65f5396-b16b-11e2-9315-00144feabdc0.html

197. Richard Engel, Robert Windrem, "How the US Oil, Gas Boom could shake up Global Order," NBCNews.com, http://worldnews.nbcnews.com/fracking; accessed May 2013.

198. Ibid.

199. Ibid.

200. Daniel Gallington, "How Fracking Could Affect U.S. Policy Towards the Middle East," *U.S. News and World Report*, December 24, 2012, http://www.usnews.com/opinion/blogs/world-report/2012/12/24/fracking-opec-and-violence-in-the-middle-east; accessed May 2013.

201. "What is Globalization?" http://www.globalization101.org/What_is_Globalization.html?PHPSESSID=e54636b5a846c31e34b20315060d2a71; accessed August 2009.

202. Benjamin Netanyahu, Translation, Prime Minister's Office, July 28, 2009; http://www.pmo.gov.il/PMOEng/Communication/PMSpeaks/speechmabal280709.htm; accessed August 2009.

203. Sam Sokol, "Steinitz: Iran Equal to 30 North Koreas," *The Jerusalem Post*, April 29, 2013, http://www.jpost.com/Diplomacy-and-Politics/Steinitz-Iran-equal-to-30-nuclear-N-Koreas-311392; accessed May 2013.

204. Ibid.

205. Ibid.

206. Y. Mansharof, "The Loss of Syria will lead to the loss of Tehran itself," MEMRI, March 11, 2012, http://www.memri.org/report/en/0/0/0/0/108/0/7069.htm; accessed May 2013.

207. "Israel complains to UN about rearming Hezbollah," http://www.reuters.com/article/2012/12/20/us-lebanon-un-israel-idUSBRE8BJ1D220121220; accessed May 2013.

208. Joseph Klein, "Syria Learns: don't Cross Israel's Red Line," *FrontLinemag.com*, May 6, 2013, http://frontpagemag.com/2013/joseph-klein/syria-learns-dont-cross-israels-red-line/comment-page-1/; accessed May 2013.

209. Voice of America, "US Military Commander Warns of Iran-Hezbollah Influence in Latin America." Voice of America, March 17, 2009, http://www.voanews.com/english/news/a-13-2009-03-17-voa44-68678507.html; accessed February 2012.

210. Elior Levy, "Nasrallah vows to free occupied Syrian Golan," *YNet Israel News*, May 9, 2013, http://www.ynetnews.com/articles/0,7340,L-4378444,00.html; accessed May 2013.

211. Ibid.

212. "Teen critically injured in attack on Negev bus," *Ynet Israel News*, April 7, 2011.

213. Daniel 10:13, NKJV

214. "Pentagon bulks up 'bunker buster' to combat Iran," Iran Focus, May 7, 2013, http://www.iranfocus.com/en/index.php?option=com_content&id=27556:pentagon-bulks-up-bunker-buster-bomb-to-combat-iran&Itemid=45; accessed May 2013.

215. *The Treasury of Scripture Knowledge: Five Hundred Thousand Scripture References and Parallel Passages*, Ezekiel 39:11 (Oak Harbor, WA: Logos Research Systems, Inc., 1995).

BOOKS BY: MIKE EVANS

Israel: America's Key to Survival

Save Jerusalem

The Return

Jerusalem D.C.

Purity and Peace of Mind

Who Cries for the Hurting?

Living Fear Free

I Shall Not Want

Let My People Go

Jerusalem Betrayed

Seven Years of Shaking: A Vision

The Nuclear Bomb of Islam

Jerusalem Prophecies

Pray For Peace of Jerusalem

America's War: The Beginning of the End

The Jerusalem Scroll

The Prayer of David

The Unanswered Prayers of Jesus

God Wrestling

Why Christians Should Support Israel

The American Prophecies

Beyond Iraq: The Next Move

The Final Move beyond Iraq

Showdown with Nuclear Iran

Jimmy Carter: The Liberal Left and World Chaos

Atomic Iran

Cursed

Betrayed

The Light

Corrie's Reflections & Meditations (booklet)

GAMECHANGER SERIES:
GameChanger
Samson Option
The Four Horsemen

THE PROTOCOLS SERIES:
The Protocols
The Candidate

The Revolution

The Final Generation

Seven Days

The Locket

Living in the F.O.G.

Persia: The Final Jihad

Jerusalem

The History of Christian Zionism

Countdown

COMING IN 2013:

Born Again: Israel's Rebirth

Ten Boom

TO PURCHASE, CONTACT: orders@timeworthybooks.com
P. O. BOX 30000, PHOENIX, AZ 85046